YAIR ZAKOVITCH

"AND YOU SHALL TELL YOUR SON..."

YAIR ZAKOVITCH

"AND YOU SHALL TELL YOUR SON..."

The Concept of the Exodus in the Bible

THE MAGNES PRESS, THE HEBREW UNIVERSITY, JERUSALEM

Published with the assistance of
The Ada G. and Leon H. Miller Memorial Endowment Fund

Distributed by The Magnes Press, P.O.B. 7695, Jerusalem 91076

ISBN 965-223-780-9
Printed in Israel

Preface

In the academic year 1988-89, I conducted a graduate seminar on the Concept of the Exodus in the Department of Biblical Studies at the Hebrew University of Jerusalem. The discussions that developed in that class helped to scatter the fog, to sharpen my understanding of the Exodus, and to formulate my ideas more clearly; the challenge of having to explain oneself to a thinking audience always contributes much to the quality of what is later written down. In the same vein, it would be difficult to imagine the crystallization of this book without the endless conversations I have enjoyed with my friend and colleague Avigdor Shinan.

Ora L. Wiskind edited the first draft of this book; Eric Zakim read through the entire manuscript with great care; my thanks go to both of them. My appreciation is also due to Oron Joffe who helped enormously with all computer-related problems.

Finally, I would like to thank the Chairman of the Academic Committee of Magnes Press, Professor Reuven Yaron, for his careful reading of the manuscript and the helpful comments he offered, and also Dan Benovici, Director of the Magnes Press, who was very encouraging and helpful in the process of publication.

I am gratefully aware that, with this book, I am able to observe the commandment, "And you shall tell your son on that day, 'It is because of what the Lord did for me when I went free from Egypt' " (Ex. 13, 8).

Y. Z.

Jerusalem
Passover Night 5751

Contents

Introduction

We read in the Passover Haggadah: "Therefore, even if we were all sages, all men of understanding, all advanced in years, and all expert in the Torah, it would yet be our duty to tell of the departure from Egypt, and the more a man tells about the departure from Egypt, the more praiseworthy he is." Recognition of this command is already evident in the Bible itself. No other event in the history of Israel is given so much attention by biblical writers as is the Exodus—as many as one hundred and twenty references in a variety of literary genres including narrative, law, prophecy and psalm, as well as extensive coverage in the Pentateuch.[1] The story of the Creation is no less vital,[2] but the account of the Exodus extends through many more chapters, from the beginning of the Book of Exodus until the end of Deuteronomy.

A number of considerations suggest that the story of the Exodus ends only when the Israelites enter the land of Canaan:

a. The ultimate purpose of the Exodus is the return to Canaan (see, for example, Ex. 3, 8, 17; 6, 6-8).

b. The life story of Moses, leader of the Exodus, begins at the very beginning of the book of Exodus, and ends when the Israelites prepare to cross the Jordan, at the very end of the book of Deuteronomy.

c. Two miracles of crossing bodies of water provide the frame-work enclosing the Exodus story: the parting of the Sea of Reeds (Ex. 14-15) and the parting of the Jordan River (Jos. 1; 3-4).[3] Psalm 114, which begins with the words, "When Israel

---

1 See Y. Hoffmann, *The Doctrine of the Exodus in the Bible*, Tel-Aviv 1983, p. 11 (Hebrew).
2 See pp. 100-105.
3 See pp. 61-62.

went forth from Egypt,"[4] indeed mentions both partings: "The sea saw them and fled, Jordan ran backward" (vs. 5); and also Psalm 66, 6: "He turned the sea into dry land; they crossed the river on foot . . . "

d. The Pentateuch itself considers the journey in the desert as an integral element of the Exodus: " . . . in order that they may see the bread that I fed you in the wilderness when I brought you out from the land of Egypt" (Ex. 16, 32); "These are the decrees, laws and rules that Moses addressed to the people of Israel, when they had left Egypt, beyond the Jordan, in the valley of Beth-peor . . . " (Dt. 4, 45-46; see also 23, 4-5; 24, 9; 25, 17). The covenant made by God with Israel in the wilderness is also a part of the Exodus: " . . . Because they forsook the covenant that the Lord, God of their fathers, made with them when He freed them from the land of Egypt" (Dt. 29, 24; see Jer. 31, 31-32). A new period begins only with the entrance to Canaan: "And everyone who saw it cried out, 'Never has such a thing happened or been seen from the day the Israelites came out of the land of Egypt [i.e., from the entrance to Canaan] to this day'" (Jud. 19, 30; see also 1 Sam. 8, 8; 2 Sam. 7, 6; 1 Ki. 8, 16, 21).

The imprint of the Exodus on biblical historiography is secured by the many covert allusions to it within the Bible. These 'quiet' references lurk in accounts of other events, which were fashioned on the literary pattern of the Exodus, and in the biographies of biblical characters which were modelled after Moses.[5] If we wish to understand and appreciate the richness and variety of expressions and conceptions of the Exodus idea throughout the Bible, we must listen not only to

4   All quotations from the Bible follow *Tanakh. The Holy Scriptures. The New JPS Translation According to the Traditional Hebrew Text*, Philadelphia 1988. I have altered the translation in certain cases where the translation was not literal enough for my purposes.
5   See Chapter Two.

the main current that flows vigorously, but also to the marginal streams of traditions, whose ideas were rejected. Recognition of these other sources will help to create a more realistic picture of the ideological arena of the biblical period.

According to Joshua 24, for instance, the Israelites worshipped the local gods of Egypt (vs. 14; see also Ez. 20, 7-8),[6] and the law was not given to them in the wilderness, by Moses, but only when they had returned to the land of Israel, by Joshua, after all alien gods had been discarded (vss. 16-26). We find a tradition that recounts the Egyptians' endurance of plagues in the wilderness (1 Sam. 4, 8); another portrays Moses as the father of a line of priests (Jud. 18, 30);[7] while yet another reveals Moses and Aaron bringing the Israelites to Canaan: " . . . and the Lord sent Moses and Aaron, who brought your fathers out of Egypt and they settled them (וישִׁבוּם) in this place" (1 Sam. 12, 8). The reading "and [God] settled them (וַיֹשִׁבֵם)," as many manuscripts and the ancient versions read, instead of "and they settled them (וישִׁבוּם)," is but a harmonization with the dominant tradition. It is less successful, however, since, according to the main tradition, the generation of the fathers who left Egypt died in the wilderness (see Nu. 13-14).[8] In some cases it is possible to reconstruct a tradition that was rejected—such as the tradition that Moses did not die but ascended to heaven—even if its expressions are preserved only in post-biblical literature.[9]

Historical issues find no place in such a study as this one. We need not consider whether the Exodus actually took place,

---

6   See pp. 124-125.
7   See p. 91.
8   See p. 123.
9   See S. E. Loewenstamm, "The Death of Moses," *Studies on the Testament of Abraham*, ed. G. W. E. Nickelsburg Jr., Montana 1976, pp. 185-217.

who left Egypt, or in what numbers. It is a different history altogether that engages us: the history of ideas.[10]

The Exodus has provided a challenge to numerous scholars and has been examined from every possible angle. It has contributed a bumper crop to our libraries.[11] I have no intention either to summarize or to repeat what is already common knowledge. My inquiry will thus focus on only three issues: The first chapter will consider a question the Bible does not answer overtly: Why were the Israelites enslaved in Egypt? The Bible explains the delay in giving the land to the children of Israel—"for the iniquity of the Amorites is not yet complete" (Gen. 15, 16)—but it does not explain why they had to be oppressed for four hundred years while waiting for the country to be evacuated (vs. 13). A variety of covert explanations offered by the Bible will be revealed in the first chapter, which will introduce us to the phenomenon of inner-biblical interpretation.

In the second chapter the many faces of the Exodus pattern in the Bible will be described[12]—the myriad covert allusions to the Exodus narrative easily detectable in the formation of periods and events that take place before and after the Exodus. Other manifestations of the Exodus will be exposed in the life stories of figures resembling Moses. By presenting their lives as antithetical to Moses, the Bible criticizes some biblical characters, while we find hidden admiration for others that the Bible has tried to suppress, such as Jeroboam, son of Nebat. The main objective of this chapter is to present the enormous dimensions of the phenomenon and the sophisticated use of the pattern.

10　For my approach to historical issues, see "Story versus History in the Bible," *Proceedings of the Eighth World Congress of Jewish Studies—Panel Sessions, Bible Studies and Hebrew Language,* Jerusalem 1983, pp. 47-60.

11　See Hoffmann (n. 1), pp. 195-211.

12　See D. Daube, *The Exodus Pattern in the Bible,* London 1963.

In the third chapter we will suggest some reasons why the Exodus reached such gigantic dimensions, why the Israelite religion needs the myth of the Exodus, and why this particular chapter in the history of Israel is appropriate for the giving of the Law. A presentation of the Exodus as serving the separatist vision of "there is a people that dwells apart" (Nu. 23, 9) and as supplying fuel for the monotheistic revolution will close the volume.

Guillaume Postel, "The Wanderings of the Children of Israel from Egypt to Canaan (following Numbers 33)", *The Bible*, London, Richard Harrison, 1562 (Eran Laor Cartographic Collection, The Jewish National and University Library)

CHAPTER ONE

Why Were the Israelites Enslaved in Egypt?
A Chapter in Inner-biblical Interpretation

A

"In the beginning there was the Word" (John 1, 1), which was immediately followed by its interpretation: the beginnings of biblical interpretation can be found within the Bible itself.[1] Inner-biblical interpretation is the light one biblical text sheds on another. The interpreting verse is used either to solve a difficulty in the interpreted text, or to adapt the interpreted text to the interpreter's own ideas. The interpreting text may be found far from the interpreted one, close to it, or even incorporated in it.

In this chapter I will not deal with overt inner-biblical interpretation—those verses which openly discuss another text or event (relating, for example, to past events in a speech or historical psalm). Rather, our focus will be on the covert variety: those occurences of inner-biblical interpretation perceptible only to the reader sensitive to the hints and allusions left by redactors, compilers and interpolators who have incorporated a literary unit into a wider context, or have woven in

---

1   See M. Fishbane's important book, *Biblical Interpretation in Ancient Israel*, Oxford 1985.

something of their own in order to present the unit in a new light.[2]

In this chapter, we will illustrate the different modes of inner-biblical interpretation by uncovering the various interpretations that the Bible offers for the enslavement of the Israelites in Egypt as well as for the agony they had to suffer in that exile. Each of these modes follows the principle of 'measure for measure.'[3]

B

The Egyptian bondage and the Exodus are mentioned overtly for the first time in the book of Genesis 15, the story of the covenant between the pieces. Yet the narrator avoids mentioning the name of the oppressing people, thereby imprinting the story with a presage of the distant future, the exact details of which remain misty:[4] "And He said to Abram, 'Know well that your offspring shall be strangers in a land not theirs, and they shall be enslaved and oppressed four hundred years; but I will execute judgement on the nation they shall serve, and in the end they shall go free with great wealth . . . And they shall return here in the fourth generation for the iniquity of the Amorites is not yet complete' " (vss. 13-16). The reference

2   See Y. Zakovitch, "Towards Characterization of the Covert Inner-Biblical Interpretation" in *Studies in Bible and Talmud*, ed. by S. Japhet, Jerusalem 1987, pp. 55-67 (Hebrew).

3   On the frequency of this ideological-literary principle in different biblical genres, see S. E. Loewenstamm, "Measure for Measure," in *Biblical Encyclopaedia* 4, pp. 840-846 (Hebrew); in rabbinic literature see: I. Heinemann, *Darkhe ha-Aggada*, Jerusalem 1954, pp. 64-70 (Hebrew).

4   For allusions to the Exodus literary complex in the covenant scene (vss. 9-12) and in the message that follows it (vss. 13-16), see below p. 60 and Y. Zakovitch, *For Three and For Four*, Jerusalem 1979, pp. 150-157 (Hebrew).

to the sin of the Amorites (vs. 16) serves to answer the question why the fulfillment of God's promise to give the land to the Israelites was postponed; the rule of God is just, and inheriting the land or being expelled from it is not the product of God's arbitrariness but a direct result of the inhabitants' behavior— an obvious hint to the children of Israel that their peaceful life in the land of Canaan depends completely on their obedience to God. God's promise to the Israelites, then, is not unconditional.

God's just providence will be expressed in the punishment of the oppressors of the Israelites—"but I will execute judgement on the nation they shall serve" (vs. 14)—as well as in Israel's compensation—"and in the end they shall go free with great wealth" (ibid.), which justifies Israel's borrowing objects of silver and gold from their Egyptian neighbors when they leave that country (Ex. 3, 22; 12, 35).[5] The importance of the concept of retribution evidenced in this paragraph prompts one unanswered question: Why did the Israelites deserve such a long and cruel oppression? (Great wealth is certainly not fair compensation for four hundred years of servitude!) The reader of the Scriptures will find no explicit answer to this question, neither in Genesis nor in the entire Bible. The reason for this may be that oppression is of secondary importance to redemption—oppression being a necessary experience leading to salvation which serves to show God's grace to Israel. In other instances as well, the Bible avoids relating suffering to God; instead, it mentions not the reason for the suffering, but the grace of God that puts an end to the distress. In the book of Ruth, for example, we read: "... there was a famine in the land" (1, 1), as if the famine happened incidentally. When the famine finally comes to an end, however, Naomi hears

---

5   A Hebrew slave is also not set free empty-handed (Dt. 15, 13-14); the argumentation makes use of the Egyptian bondage (vs. 15); see D. Daube, *The Exodus Pattern in the Bible*, London 1963, pp. 55-61.

" . . . that the Lord had taken note of His people and given them food" (vs. 6).[6]

The same reason may explain why the Bible's description of the Israelites' oppression is limited to a few details at the beginning of the book of Exodus. These verses reveal the circumstances which led the Egyptians to enslave the Israelites, while they omit any explanation of why the Israelites had been doomed to such a cruel fate in the first place. What we do know of the oppression of the Israelites is, for the most part, gathered from the descriptions of the various stages of redemption, beginning with the moment God showed himself to Moses in the burning bush (Ex. 3, 7). Faced with such a paucity of information, we must ask ourselves whether explanations for the bondage of the Israelites in Egypt are given, instead, in a covert or indirect way and, if so, what these explanations may be.

C

The book of Genesis recounts one descent to Egypt and return to Canaan: the story of Abraham and Sarah's journey to Egypt (Gen. 12, 10-20). This short story serves as an introduction to the history of Israel in their exile in Egypt and their subsequent Exodus from there. Each stage of this story finds a parallel in the story of the Egyptian bondage, while a comparison of the expressions common to the two narratives makes clear that the relationship is conscious and intentional.[7]

6   See also Genesis 12, 10; 26, 1, 12 (but according to 2 Kings 8, 1 the famine was brought by God).
7   See U. Cassuto, *Commentary on Genesis*, vol. 2, Jerusalem 1964, pp. 334-337.

Genesis 12	The history of Israel in Egypt
...and Abram went down to Egypt (vs. 10)	So ten of Joseph's brothers went down ... [to] Egypt (Gen. 42, 3; see also 43, 15; Nu. 20, 15)
to sojourn there (vs. 10)	We have come to sojourn in this land (Gen. 47, 4; see also Isa. 52, 4)
for the famine was severe in the land (vs. 10)	But the famine in the land was severe (Gen. 43, 1; see also 47, 4)
they will kill me and let you live (vs. 12)	if it is a boy, kill him; if it is a girl, let her live (Ex. 1, 16; see also vs. 22)
that I may remain alive thanks to you (vs. 13)	... it was to save life that God sent me ahead of you ... and to save your lives in an extraordinary deliverance (Gen. 45, 5, 7)
When Abram entered Egypt (vs. 14)	These are the names of the sons of Israel who came to Egypt (Ex. 1, 1)
But the Lord afflicted Pharaoh ... with mighty afflictions (vs. 17)	I will bring one more affliction upon Pharaoh (Ex. 11, 1)
Pharaoh sent for Abram (vs. 18)	Then Pharaoh sent for Moses and Aaron (Ex. 8, 4; see also 8, 21; 9, 27)
... take [her] and be gone (vs. 19)	Take ... as you said, and be gone (Ex. 12, 32)
... and they sent him off with his wife (vs. 20)	Now when Pharaoh sent off the people (Ex. 13, 17)

19

Now Abram was very rich in cattle, silver and gold (13, 2)	Each woman shall borrow from her neighbor and the lodger in her house objects of silver and gold . . . (Ex. 3, 22; see also 12, 35)

As the following Midrash points out, the journey of the patriarch to Egypt represents a striking example of the common pattern, "like father like son":

> R. Phinehas commented in R. Hoshaya's name: The Holy One, blessed be He, said to our father Abraham, "Go forth and tread out a path for thy children." For you find that everything written in connection with Abraham is written in connection with his children . . . [*Genesis Rabbah* (London-New York 1983), 40, 6 (p. 330)]

But what is the meaning behind the pattern aside from the opportunity it gives to enumerate in detail all the similarities between the histories of the father and his sons? It seems to me that the impression of repetition or even periodicity in history is created to teach that the world is not governed by chance but by a well defined plan, discernable in patterns set by divine providence. Temporariness and uniqueness may be frightening; to believe the world is governed by its God and creator, and the future foreseeable according to past events, awakens confidence. The chronicles of the patriarchs are thus like a detailed table of contents; they are an overview at the beginning of the book of the history of Israel. Just as Abraham entered Egypt safely and left it safely, so did his children, and so the children of Israel will survive other calamities awaiting them, such as the Babylonian exile.

But aside from the positive psychological effects of Genesis 12, 10-20, we should remark on how this short story is interpreted in the Bible itself. Abraham's descent to Egypt does not meet with approval in Genesis 26. The storyteller explicitly mentions the hunger in Abraham's days, thereby signalling to the reader that a comparison between the behavior of Isaac and his father is appropriate. He makes it clear that Abraham's descent to Egypt was a choice the patriarch made without the approval of God. "There was a famine in the land— aside from the previous famine that had occurred in the days of Abraham—and Isaac went to Abimelech king of the Philistines, in Gerar. The Lord had appeared to him and said: Do not go down to Egypt; stay in the land which I point out to you . . . " (vss. 1-2). Does the narrator presume the immediate descent of Abraham to Egypt—as soon as he encountered his first difficulty after reaching Canaan—to have been a sin? Abraham's decision to leave the country was not initiated by God but by Abraham himself. Abraham had not even bothered to call on God, pray to him or ask for his guidance. God thus has to warn Isaac not to repeat his father's mistake when he faces a similar problem.

When God wants someone to descend to Egypt he makes himself very clear: before Jacob leaves Canaan for Egypt, he stops in Beer-Sheba and offers "Sacrifices *to the God of his father Isaac*" (Gen. 46, 1), well aware of God's earlier prohibition to his father, and God appears to him in his dream—the one and only revelation in the Joseph narrative—and tells him: "I am God, *the God of your father*. Fear not to go down to Egypt, for I will make you there into a great nation. I myself will go down with you to Egypt, and I myself will also bring you back . . . " (vss. 3-4).[8]

The Midrash indeed draws the connection between the ad hoc permission to Jacob and the prohibition to Isaac, and makes it clear that God's prohibition to his father provided the impetus for Jacob's sacrifices:

"And he said I am God, the God of your father. Fear not to go down to Egypt" (Gen. 46, 3). Jacob, our father, said: My father wanted to descend to Egypt and was told by the

8   The Septuagint to verse 3 reads the plural form, "your fathers," but the Masoretic text is to be preferred.

Holy One, blessed be He, "Do not go down to Egypt" (Gen. 26, 2), so I, how do I go down? Therefore: "He offered sacrifices to the God of his father Isaac" (46, 1) because He stopped his father from going down to Egypt and Jacob was commanded to descend. The evidence for this is that the Holy One blessed be He told him, " 'Fear not to go down to Egypt'; although I have stopped your father from descending, you go down." [*Midrash Lekah Tov to Genesis*, p. 221]

The prohibition to Isaac in Genesis 26 caused Nahmanides to understand Abraham's descent as a sin for which his children must pay, something like 'Parents have eaten sour grapes and children's teeth are blunted' (Jer. 31, 29): "His leaving the land, concerning which he had been commanded from the beginning, on account of the famine, was also a sin he committed, for in famine God would redeem him from death. It was because of this deed that the exile in the land of Egypt at the hand of Pharaoh was decreed for his children. In the place of justice, there is wickedness and sin" [Ramban (Nahmanides), *Commentary on the Torah: Genesis*, trans. C. B. Chavel, (New York 1971), on Gen. 12, 10 (pp. 173-174)]. Genesis 12, 10-20 serves, according to Nahmanides, as an explanation for the question left unanswered in chapter 15—why the Israelites suffered in Egypt. Nahmanides' answer reveals the intention of the compiler of the book of Genesis.[9]

9   Nahmanides does not hesitate to mention the patriarchs' sins (see below, his note on Gen. 15, 6); see M. H. Segal, *Parshanut ha-Mikra*, Jerusalem 1971, p. 101 (Hebrew). Nahmanides' approach challenges the old and well documented idea that the famine was indeed one of the tests Abraham underwent and passed. This approach is expressed already in the book of Jubilees 17, 17: "But the Lord knew that Abraham was faithful in all his afflictions; for he had tested him through his country and with famine..." Following *Pirke Avot* 5, 3—"With ten trials Abraham our father was tried, and he bore them all to make known how great was the love of Abraham our father" (trans. by R. T. Herford, New York 1962)—some midrashim specify the ten tests, including: "The fourth test, from the day heaven and earth were created

The Abraham story adds new dimensions to other details in the Exodus narrative.[10] For example, Abraham fears for his own life, " . . . they will *kill me* and *let you live*" (12, 12), and his fear leads him to let his wife be taken by the Egyptians. For this behavior, he, in the form of his children, will be punished 'measure for measure': their male infants are to be killed and the female ones left alive, "Every boy that is born you shall throw in the Nile, but *let* every girl *live*" (Ex. 1, 22).

Not only verse 22 relates to the story of Abraham and Sarah in Egypt: there is a clear interrelationship between the entire midwives' story (Ex. 1, 15-22) and Genesis 12, 10-20. Awareness of this sheds light on both narratives:

a. Abraham fears for his life and knows his wife is not in danger: "They will kill me and let you live" (vs. 12); Pharaoh commands all the male newborns to be killed: " . . . if it is a boy, kill him; if it is a girl, let her live" (vs. 16; see also vs. 22).

b. Abraham expects good fortune as the result of his lie: " . . . *that it may go well with me* because of you" (vs. 13); "And because of her *it went well with Abram*; he acquired sheep, oxen, asses, male and female slaves, she asses, and camels" (vs. 16); God treats the midwives with favor because they dared disobey the king: "*And God dealt well with the midwives*" (vs. 20a). The midrash calls attention to this similarity:

> there was no famine but in the days of Abraham, and not in all the countries but only in the land of Canaan, to test him, to bring him down to Egypt" (*Pirke de-Rabbi Eliezer*, ch. 26).

10 The Abraham story has two close parallels in the book of Genesis (20; 26, 1-13) but only our story takes place in Egypt while the other two, which interpret and refine Genesis 12, 10-20, take place in the court of Abimelech, king of Gerar. See S. Sandmel, "The Haggada within Scripture," *JBL* 80 (1961), pp. 105-122; A. Shinan and Y. Zakovitch, *Abram and Sarai in Egypt*, Research Projects of the Institute of Jewish Studies, Monograph Series 2, Jerusalem 1983, pp. 133-138 (Hebrew).

> For you find everything written in connection to Abraham
> is written in connection with his children . . . Abraham:
> Say, I pray thee, that thou art my sister, that it may go
> well with me; Israel: And God dealt well with the mid-
> wives. [*Genesis Rabbah* (see p. 20), 40, 6]

Verse 20a, however, "And God dealt well with the midwives," duplicates verse 21, which explains how God favored
the two women and granted them a 'measure for measure' reward: the increase of their families: "And because the midwives feared God, He established households for them." It
also disturbs the natural continuity between the midwives'
deed and its consequence: "and the people multiplied and increased greatly." We posit, then, that verse 20a "and God
dealt well with the midwives," makes up a secondary addition intended to assimilate the Exodus story to the similar one
in Genesis.[11] The addition, like many other secondary elements, did not find its way to the right place,[12] after the words
"And because the midwives feared God," lodging instead in
the previous verse.

c. Because of Abraham's lie, Pharaoh sends for him, asking
for an explanation: "Pharaoh sent for Abram and said to him,
'Why have you done this thing . . . ' " (vs. 18). In the Samaritan Pentateuch the words "the king of Egypt" in Exodus 1, 18
are replaced by the word "Pharaoh," another assimilation
with the parallel verse in Genesis.

These similarities serve to invite the reader to compare the
two stories, a comparison which alerts one to the following:

a. Abraham lies in order to save his own life, for which he
is ready to abandon his wife. The midwives, in contrast to
Abraham, fool the king and later even lie to him (vs. 19) in
order to save the lives of the Hebrew male newborns.

11 See Y. Zakovitch, "Assimilation in Biblical Narratives" in
    Empirical Models for Biblical Criticism, ed. J. Tigay,
    Philadelphia 1985, pp. 175-196.
12 See, for example, Gen. 10, 12, 14.

b. In his distress, Abraham does not rely on God's help, in contrast to the midwives who fear God (vs. 17).

c. When Pharaoh calls for Abraham, the patriarch has nothing to say; his silence signifies his assent. The midwives, on the other hand, do not hesitate to answer falsely to the king for their noble cause.

d. Pharaoh is the one who favors Abraham, and improves his financial position, while it is God who favors the midwives.

The contrast between the two stories emphasizes once again Abraham's undignified behavior, behavior which warranted punishment.

The gap between Abraham's negative deeds and the positive deed of the midwives widens even more when we realize that, in the original version of the story, the midwives were not Hebrew (vs. 15), but Egyptian: verses 16 and 19 make it clear that the midwives do not deliver Hebrew babies exclusively. It would have been more natural for Pharaoh to expect the cooperation of Egyptian women than Hebrew women. In fact, the God-fearing of the midwives and their reward can be astonishing *only* if they are foreigners. (On the God-fearing of gentiles see, for instance, Jonah 1, 16; Job 1, 9.) The story which follows the story of the midwives (2, 1-10) continues the same theme: it tells of Pharaoh's daughter who saves Moses. God seems to look on with a smile as Pharaoh's plans are stymied by his own people—even by his own daughter.

That the midwives are foreign is clear in the Septuagint of verse 15. Instead of "to the Hebrew midwives," we read there: "to the midwives *of* the Hebrews" (see also the Vulgate). Josephus Flavius also knows the midwives as foreigners: "He [the king] commanded that . . . the Egyptian midwives should watch the labors of the Hebrew women, and observe what is born, for those were the women who were enjoined to do the office of midwives to them; and by reason of their relation to the

25

king would not transgress his commands" (*Ant.* 2, 9, 2).[13] The Egyptian midwives become more positive figures than Abraham the Hebrew! In fact, it seems that the Masoretic rendering, "to the Hebrew midwives," reflects a later stage in the text's transmission, when there was no longer tolerance for the idea of foreigners' God-fearing—especially Egyptians—or of their role in Israel's salvation.[14]

D

The juxtaposition of stories, achieved by placing two stories one after the other, is a tool the compiler uses to tell the reader how he wants the stories to be read. Each individual story may contain its own message, but its placement in the wider context of the historiographic mosaic gives it a new meaning which serves a broader purpose.[15] Keeping this in mind, we shall now move on to examine another explanation for the Egyptian bondage offered by the compiler of Genesis.

The story following the news of the Egyptian bondage is in chapter 16. That chapter opens with Hagar the Egyptian: "Sarai, Abram's wife, had borne him no children. She had an Egyptian maidservant whose name was Hagar" (vs. 1).

13 Some of the modern commentators discuss the possibility that the midwives were of Egyptian nationality. See, for instance H. Holzinger, *Exodus (KHAT)*, Tübingen 1900, p. 3; B. S. Childs, *Exodus (OTL)*, London 1974, p. 16.

14 On reducing the role of the Gentiles in the process of Israel's redemption see, for example, the different biblical Balaam traditions (A. Rofé, *The Book of Balaam [Numbers 22, 2-24, 25]*, Jerusalem 1979 [Hebrew]). The tradition about Moses' father-in-law went through a similar process, see pp. 117-118.

15 On the importance of juxtaposition in the Bible as a meaningful editorial device, see A. Shinan, Y. Zakovitch, "Midrash on Scripture and Midrash within Scripture," *Scripta Hierosolymitana* 31, *Studies in Bible*, edited by S. Japhet, Jerusalem 1986, pp. 267-270; Y. Zakovitch (n. 2), pp. 60-64.

Hagar's nationality is mentioned again in verse 3, thereby assuring the reader's attention to this detail. Chapter 15 discusses the Israelites' oppression in Egypt: " . . . and they shall be enslaved and *oppressed* four hundred years" (15, 13), while in chapter 16 we hear of Hagar's oppression in Abraham's house: "Then Sarai *oppressed* her" (16, 6); "And the angel of the Lord said to her, go back to your mistress and *be oppressed by her*" (vs. 9). Abraham is promised numberless offspring: " . . . none but your very own issue shall be your heir . . . Look toward heaven and count the stars, if you are able to count them. And he added, so shall your offspring be" (15, 4-5). Hagar, who carries Abraham's son, Ishmael, in her womb, receives a similar promise: "I will greatly increase your offspring and they shall be too many to count" (16, 10).

Clearly, then, there is an intentional relationship between these two adjacent chapters, but we have yet to uncover its meaning. Let us examine the striking parallels between Genesis 16 and the history of the Israelites in Egypt:

a. Hagar is oppressed in Abraham's house (vss. 6, 9) and the Israelites are oppressed in Egypt, as we learn not only from Genesis 15, 13, but also from the enslavement story in the book of Exodus: "So they set taskmasters over them to *oppress* them with forced labor . . . But the more they were *oppressed*, the more they increased and spread out . . . " (1, 11-12). Compare also Deuteronomy 26, 6: "The Egyptians dealt harshly with us and *oppressed* us; they imposed heavy labor upon us."[16]

b. It was the anxiety of the Egyptians over the proliferation of the Israelites that motivated the Egyptians to oppress the other nation: "so that they may not increase" (Ex. 1, 10). Sarah oppresses Hagar for the same reason, because she has lost the respect of her maidservant after she conceives: " . . . and when she saw that she had conceived, her mistress

16   The Septuagint to Genesis 15, 13 adds the words "and they will be dealt harshly with" (ויֵרְעוּ אותם) before the words "and oppressed," a harmonization with the verse in Deuteronomy.

27

was lowered in her esteem" (16, 4); "Now that she sees she is pregnant, I am lowered in her esteem" (vs. 5).

c. Hagar flees into the wilderness (vs. 7) as do the Israelites.

d. The words of the angel to Hagar, "For the Lord *has heard* your *suffering*" (an explanation of her son's name, Ishmael, vs. 11) remind us of the comforting words of God to Moses: "I have seen the *suffering* of my people in Egypt and *have heard* their outcry because of their taskmasters . . . " (Ex. 3, 7; see also 2, 24; 6; 5).[17]

e. The same geographical sites are mentioned in both stories: "in the *wilderness*, the spring on the road to *Shur*" (Gen. 16, 7); "They went out into the *wilderness of Shur*" (Ex. 15, 22); Kadesh (Gen. 16, 14; Nu. 13, 26; 20, 1, etc.).

f. In contrast to Hagar's story, in which the Egyptian maid-servant's son is adopted by the family of the Hebrew mistress, in the birth story of Moses it is the son of a slave, Moses the Hebrew, who is adopted by the daughter of Pharaoh (Ex. 2).

The striking resemblance between Hagar's story and the history of Israel in Egypt is not accidental. The message is clear: the oppression of the Israelites is a 'measure for measure' punishment for Hagar's treatment in Abraham's house. The juxtaposition of Genesis 15-16 leads to the same conclusion. Naḥmanides, whose interpretation to Genesis 12, 10-20 was cited above, also understands Abraham and Sarah's behavior toward Hagar as a sin which justifies that punishment will be visited on their children:

> "And Sarai dealt harshly with her, and she fled from her face"—Our mother did transgress by this affliction, and Abraham also, by his permitting her to do so. And so, God heard [Hagar's] affliction and gave her a son who would be "a wild ass of a man" (vs. 12), to afflict the seed of

17 Note the chiastic structure frequent in inner-biblical quotation. See M. Seidel, "Parallels between the Book of Isaiah and the Book of Psalms," *Ḥiqre Mikra*, Jerusalem 1978, pp. 1-97 (Hebrew); R. Weiss, "Chiasm in the Bible," *Studies in the Text and Language of the Bible*, Jerusalem 1981, pp. 259-274 (Hebrew).

Abraham and Sarah with all kinds of affliction.
[Naḥmanides (see above, p. 21) to 16, 6 (p. 213); cf. also
Kimḥi]

The existence of a 'measure for measure' relationship between Genesis 16 and the Egyptian bondage is further confirmed in the other Hagar story in Genesis, the account of her expulsion with her son Ishmael from Abraham's home in chapter 21:

a. This story mentions her nationality once again: "Sarah saw the son whom Hagar the Egyptian had borne to Abraham" (vs. 9).

b. Sarah's demand to *expel that slave woman and her son*" (vs. 10) reminds us of the Israelites' expulsion from Egypt: "Since they had been *expelled* from Egypt" (Ex. 12, 39; see also 6, 1; 10, 11).

c. Another expression common to the two stories is "sending away" (Gen. 21, 14; Ex. 3, 20; 4, 21, etc.).

d. Like the Israelites, Hagar leaves for the desert: "And she wandered about in the wilderness..." (vs. 14).

e. The shortage of water in Genesis, "When the water was gone from the skin..." (Gen. 21, 15), is also a frequent element in the story of the wandering of the Israelites in the wilderness "...they travelled three days in the wilderness and found no water. They came to Marah, but they could not drink the water" (Ex. 15, 22-26; see also 17, 1-7; Nu. 20, 1-13).

f. The abandonment by its mother of the thirsty child in Genesis, "She left (וַתַּשְׁלֵךְ) the child under one of the bushes" (Gen. 21, 15), finds its parallel in the throwing of the Israelite boys into the Nile: "Every boy that is born you shall throw (תַּשְׁלִיכֻהוּ) into the Nile" (Ex. 1, 22).

g. In Genesis, God opened the eyes of the thirsty maid-servant, "Then God opened her eyes and she saw a well of water" (21, 19); we compare this with Numbers 21, 16: "And from there to Beer, which is the well where the Lord said to Moses, 'Assemble the people that I may give them water.'"

h. "The Wilderness of Paran" (Gen. 21, 21) is well known from the Israelite journey through the wilderness (Nu. 10, 12; 12, 16; 13, 26, etc.).[18]

18 'Measure for measure' considerations also dictated the placement of chapter 21 between chapters 20 and 22. At the end of chapter 20 Abraham prays to God concerning Abimelech, the result being: "and God healed Abimelech and his wife and his slave girls, so that they bore children" (vs. 17). Chapter 21 thus opens with God's reward to Abraham and Sarah: "The Lord took note of Sarah as He had promised,... Sarah conceived and bore a son to Abraham in his old age" (vss. 1-2). Chapter 21 is followed by the binding of Isaac in chapter 22. There are some clear points of resemblance between the two chapters:
a. An identical phrase describes how Hagar and Ishmael are sent away and how Abraham and Isaac set out on their way: "Early next morning Abraham got up... and took..." (21, 14; 22, 3).
b. In both stories an angel intervenes, saving the child: "...an angel of God called to Hagar from heaven and said to her..." (21, 17); "Then an angel of the Lord called to him from heaven" (22, 11).
c. Following this divine intervention, the parent identifies the source for rescue: "Then God opened her eyes and she saw a well of water" (21, 19); "When Abraham looked up, his eye fell upon a ram ..." (22, 14).
d. In both stories a blessing for increase follows the rescue (21, 18; 22, 16-18).
e. Hagar wanders in the wilderness of Beer-sheba (21, 14), and Abraham returns to Beer-sheba from the site of the binding of Isaac (22, 19).
The similarity between the two narratives emphasizes their interrelationship: Abraham, who was forced against his will to send Ishmael away, must then sacrifice his beloved son Isaac; Abraham obeys God twice and passes both most difficult tests. The post-biblical literature indeed considers Abraham's experience with Hagar as one of his tests: the passage from the book of Jubilees quoted above (n. 9) continues "... and he had tested him through Ishmael and Hagar his slave girl when he sent her away. And in every test to which the Lord subjected him, he had

E

The 'measure for measure' principle is expressed once again in
the Israelite-Ishmaelite relationship in the context of the
Egyptian bondage, in the story of the selling of Joseph to the
Egyptians. This story is wrought with duplications and contra-
dictions which were convincingly explained by Loewenstamm.[19] The original stratum of the story portrayed the
brothers casting Joseph into the pit, following Reuben's advice;
the Midianites then find him and sell him to Potiphar in
Egypt (Gen. 37, 21-22; 24; 28a[a], b; 29-30). A second writer, who
was interested in emphasizing Judah's role, exchanged these
verses with his own version:

> and took him and cast him into the pit. The pit was
> empty; there was no water in it. Then they sat down to a
> meal. Looking up, they saw a caravan of Ishmaelites
> coming from Gilead, their camels bearing gum, balm, and
> ladanum to be taken to Egypt. Then Judah said to his
> brothers, What do we gain by killing our brother and cov-
> ering up his blood? Come let us sell him to the Ish-
> maelites, but let us not do away with him ourselves. After
> all he is our brother, our own flesh. His brothers agreed
> (vss. 24-27). They pulled Joseph out of the pit; they sold
> Joseph for twenty pieces of silver to the Ishmaelites, who
> brought Joseph to Egypt (vs. 28a[b]-b).

A later redactor reinserted the verses about Reuben, which had
been omitted by the Judean writer, and created the present
version of the story.[20]

been found faithful. . . " (17, 17-18); see also *Pirke de-Rabbi
Eliezer*, ch. 30.
19 S. E. Loewenstamm, "Reuben and Judah in the Joseph-Cycle,"
Fourth World Congress of Jewish Studies Papers, vol. I,
Jerusalem 1967, pp. 69-70 (Hebrew); see there his arguments
against the solutions of the documentary hypothesis.
20 The Midianites sell Joseph in the original stratum of the story so
that their crime creates a framework: the daughters of Midian

What interests us most is the secondary, Judean stratum. Its writer was concerned not only to substitute Judah for Reuben, but also to replace the Midianites with the Ishmaelites in order to make Ishmael's children the messengers of God's verdict, thereby punishing the Israelites for the mistreatment of Hagar and her son by their ancestors. Joseph is sold by the Ishmaelites to Potiphar (39, 1) and, as expected, becomes his slave (39, 17, 19; 41, 12, and see Ps. 105, 17: "He sent ahead of them a man, Joseph, sold into slavery"). Moreover, while in the original story the brothers were only indirectly involved in selling Joseph—the Midianites find him in the pit without the brothers' mediation (vs. 28a) and sell him in Egypt (vs. 36)—in the Ishmaelite stratum the brothers sell Joseph to the Ishmaelites and thus deserve the punishment of slavery.

I do not dismiss the additional possibility that Pharaoh's order to cast the male infants into the Nile, "Every boy that is born you shall throw (תשליכוהו) into the Nile . . . " (Ex. 1, 22), has its roots in the brothers' casting Joseph into the pit: " . . . and took him and cast him (וישלכו אתו) into the pit" (Gen. 37, 24).

The ugliness of the brothers' behavior is highlighted in the story told directly after Pharaoh's order—the account of Moses' birth—which is the 'reflection story' of Genesis 37.[21] In contrast to Joseph's brothers, who abandon him, Moses' sister

tempt the Israelites who wander in the wilderness (Nu. 25). The fact that the Israelite who is mentioned by name is "a chieftain of a Simeonite ancestral house" (vs. 14) may very well relate to the Joseph story: Simeon is second to Reuben in age, and Reuben, who wanted to save Joseph, is innocent. Reuben's plan to restore Joseph to his father would have succeeded had Joseph not been taken out of the pit by the Midianites (37, 22, 28a[a], 29-30). In Egypt, too, Joseph arrests Simeon (rather than Reuben) because he is aware of Reuben's good intentions (42, 24).

21 On reflection stories see Y. Zakovitch, "Reflection Stories— Another Dimension of the Evaluation of Characters in Biblical Narrative," *Tarbiz* 54 (1985), pp. 165-176 (Hebrew).

"stationed herself at a distance, to learn what would befall him" (Ex. 2, 4). When Moses is drawn out of the water by Pharaoh's daughter, his sister is nearby to ensure that his family will continue to take care of him and that he will be nursed by his own mother (vss. 7-9); Joseph's father does not know what has happened to his beloved son because his other sons lie to him (vss. 32-34).

The fact that Jacob's sons deserve a severe punishment is not contradicted by Joseph's consoling words to his brothers: "Have no fear! Am I a substitute for God? Besides, although you intended me harm, God intended it for good, so as to bring about the present result—the survival of many people!" (Gen. 50, 19-20). Joseph will not take revenge on his brothers, whose deeds follow the divine plan, but they deserve God's punishment for their sin toward Joseph.[22]

F

Thus far, the reasons offered in the Bible for the enslavement in Egypt are derived from sins committed by Abraham and by Jacob's sons in the land of Canaan. Proof that the patriarchs' sojourn in Canaan is considered a sinful period is supplied by the chronological data of the priestly document: "The length of time that the Israelites lived in Egypt was four hundred thirty years" (Ex. 12, 40). This period is twice as long as the time the patriarchs lived in Canaan: two hundred fifteen years passed between Abraham's departure from Haran and Jacob's confrontation with Pharaoh (see Gen. 12, 4; 21, 5; 25, 26;

---

22 The Jacob cycle also exemplifies the distinction between the divine plan and human sinful behavior which fits the plan yet nonetheless needs to be punished: Jacob deserved the rights of the first-born according to God's plan (Gen. 25, 23), but stealing his father's blessing forces him to escape (27, 41-45) and justifies the exchange of Rachel for Leah by their father (29, 23-26) as well as Jacob's enslavement by him (30, 25-29).

33

47, 9). Indeed, the Samaritan Pentateuch and the Septuagint share a tempting reading of Exodus 12, 40; instead of "in Egypt" they read: "in the land of Egypt and in the land of Canaan"—they divide the four hundred thirty years into two equal parts of two hundred fifteen each. Josephus Flavius states this explicitly (*Ant.* 2, 15, 2, following Demetrius the Chronographer).[23] This reading resolves the apparent contradiction between the chronological data and the same document's enumerating only four generations between Levi and Moses: Levi is the father of Kohath, the father of Amram, the father of Moses (Ex. 6, 16-18; Nu. 26, 58-59). Upon examination, other chronological data in the priestly document also fail to correspond with the exceedingly long period of four hundred thirty years in Egypt. (Levi's son, Kohath, left Canaan for Egypt [Gen. 46, 11], and he is one hundred thirty-three years old when he dies [Ex. 6, 18]; his son, Amram, dies at the age of one hundred thirty-seven [vs. 20] and his son Moses appears before Pharaoh at the age of eighty [Ex. 7, 7]; this makes a maximum total of 350 years, and that only by assuming that sons are being born on the day their fathers die.) Nevertheless, the number four hundred thirty seems to be original in describing the Egyptian exile, and the priestly writer seems unconcerned by the tension between this number and the four generations, just as the narrator of Genesis 15 is not troubled with his conflicting data: " . . . and they shall be enslaved and oppressed four hundred years" (vs. 13); "And they shall return here in the fourth generation" (vs. 16; we will return to this point below).

This two-to-one ratio, the four hundred thirty years of servitude against the two hundred fifteen in Canaan, is founded on an idea with far-reaching implications. For each year of sin, the Israelites must pay with two years in Egypt.

---

23 Y. Gutman, *The Beginnings of Jewish-Hellenistic Literature*, vol. 1, Jerusalem 1969, p. 134 (Hebrew); J. Heinemann, *Aggadah and its Development*, Jerusalem 1974, pp. 69-70 (Hebrew).

This concept finds its parallel in the words of the prophet: "Speak tenderly to Jerusalem and declare to her that her term of service is over, that her iniquity is expiated; For she has received at the hand of the Lord double for all her sins" (Isa. 40, 2; for other double-punishments see Ex. 22, 3, 6, 8; for double reward, see Job 42, 12-13).

Surprisingly, the very same period of time, four hundred thirty years, also passes between the building of Solomon's Temple (1 Ki. 6, 1) and its destruction, followed by the Babylonian exile;[24] we must seek the meaning of this non-incidental equation. On the one hand, it would be unreasonable to suppose that the priestly chronological calculations in the Pentateuch—two hundred fifteen and four hundred thirty—were created by someone who already knew the entire chronological system of the book of Kings. On the other hand, it is also illogical to think that the chronological data in Kings was artificially created in order to suit the chronology of the Pentateuch. It seems to me that the redactor who assigned the building of the temple to Solomon's fourth year (1 Ki. 6, 1 and see also vss. 37-38) was the same one who calculated and made certain that from that year to the destruction, the same number of years pass as the Israelites spent in Egypt. The equation seems to suggest that sins would no longer be forgiven once the temple was established. The existence of the temple, residence in the land of Israel, and the continuation of the Davidic line,

---

24 37 years of Solomon (40 [1 Ki. 11, 42], 3 of which passed until the temple was built); 17 of Rehoboam (14, 21); 41 of Asa (15, 10); 25 of Jehoshaphat (22, 42); 8 of Joram (2 Ki. 8, 17); 1 of Ahaziah (8, 26); 6 of Athaliah (11, 3); 40 of Jooash (12, 2); 29 of Amaziah (14, 2); 52 of Azariah (15, 2); 16 of Yotham (15, 33); 16 of Ahaz (16, 2); 29 of Hezekiah (18, 2); 55 of Manasseh (21, 1); 2 of Amon (21, 19); 31 of Josiah (22, 1); 3 months of Johoahaz (which are not taken into account [23, 31]); 11 of Jehoiakim (23, 36); 3 months of Johoiachin (which are not taken into account [24, 8]); 11 of Zedekiah (24, 18). See N. Sarna, *Exploring Exodus*, New York 1987, p. 9.

all would depend on observance of the Law (see for instance 1 Ki. 8, 25; 9, 6-9). God would be patient with Israel for four hundred and thirty years, for as many years as they were in Egypt—for as many years as he was patient with the Amorites until their iniquity was full (Gen. 15, 16) at which time he removed them from their land and gave it to the Israelites. If the Israelites continue to sin, they, too, will be removed from the land—and that is what indeed took place according to the redactor of the book of Kings.

A concept of retribution exists in the chronological system of Genesis 15 as well. God is patient with the Amorites until the fourth generation, a length of time consistent with other instances: "Visiting the guilt of the parents upon the children, upon the third and upon the fourth generation . . . " (Ex. 20, 5; 34, 7; Nu. 14, 18; Dt. 5, 9).[25] If the Pentateuch indeed promotes the concept that the children of Israel are punished in Egypt for the sin of their forefathers, then in their case, too, God enacts the rule of "visiting the guilt of the fathers . . . "—but, in this case, it is the flip side of this rule: their fourth generation will return to Canaan! The link between Genesis 15, 16 and the verses about "visiting the guilt . . . " is recognized already by the Sages: " ' . . . the fourth generation,' to fulfill what is said in the Scriptures: 'visiting the guilt of the parents . . . upon the third and upon the fourth generations' " (*Midrash Agada*, ed. S. Buber, Vienna 1894, p. 34).

G

Calling the Egyptian bondage "the iron blast furnace" (Dt. 4, 20; 1 Ki. 8, 51; Jer. 11, 4) testifies to the idea that the Israelites were purged in Egypt of their sins. After recalling Israel's sins (Isa. 48, 8), the prophet Isaiah speaks of their punishment,

25 For the three-four literary numerical pattern in expressions of retribution, see Y. Zakovitch (n. 4), pp. 175-227.

using terms strongly reminiscent of the Egyptian chapter in their history: "See, I refine you, but not as silver; I test you in the furnace of affliction" (vs. 10). (On the figurative use of "furnace" to relay the idea of severe punishment, see also Ez. 22, 17-22.) Refining, even without mentioning the word "furnace," signifies a test (Ps. 17, 3; 66, 10) which almost always entails a punishment (Isa. 1, 25; Jer. 6, 29; 9, 6; Zec. 13, 9; Dan. 11, 35; 12, 10).[26]

More indirect evidence for the concept that the Egyptian servitude is a punishment for sins committed in Canaan may be found in God's threat to punish the children of Israel by returning them to Egypt: "The Lord will send you back to Egypt in galleys, by a route which I told you you should not see again. Then you shall offer yourselves for sale to your enemies as male and female slaves, but none will buy" (Dt. 28, 68). This future punishment is to be even more severe than the former: no one will even buy them as slaves so that they will have no means of subsistence.

The prophet Hosea also presents the return to Egypt as a punishment: " . . . Behold, he remembers their iniquity, he will punish their sins: back to Egypt with them" (8, 13), and see also 9, 1-3: "Rejoice not, O Israel, as other peoples exult; for you have strayed away from your God . . . But Ephraim shall return to Egypt and shall eat unclean food in Assyria." If the future return to Egypt is considered a punishment, then projection in retrospect is unavoidable: their past Egyptian bondage was a punishment as well.

Finally, other examples of the Exodus literary type also depict the Egyptian exile as a punishment: in the story of Jacob in Haran and his subjugation to Laban (Gen. 29-31), a story

---

26 It is interesting that in Psalm 105 the poet who tells about the selling of Joseph juxtaposes iron—the yoke on Joseph's neck—to his refining: "His feet were subjected to fetters; an iron collar was put on his neck. Until his prediction came true the decree of the Lord refined him" (vss. 18-19).

which follows the Exodus pattern,[27] Jacob is forced to leave
Canaan first of all because he has usurped the blessing des-
tined for his brother (Gen. 27, 42-45). In another example, the
Ark of God was captured by the Philistines (1 Sam. 5, 1-6, 16)
as a punishment to the children of Israel for the sins of the
priests, the sons of Eli (note the overt references to the Exodus
narrative in 4, 8; 6, 6).[28] The punishment motif in these
parallel stories seems to derive from the writers' understanding of the servitude element in the Exodus story.

H

Abraham's sins in Canaan (sections C-D) justify the subjugation of all the children of Israel in Egypt, while the behavior
of Jacob's sons towards their brother Joseph (section E) justifies
their servitude, but not Joseph's; only Joseph's own sin can explain why his sons shared a common lot with all the other
Israelites. Joseph's sin relates to his treatment of his brothers
and the Egyptians during the years of hunger, treatment
which clearly demonstrated a double standard. The brothers
enjoyed luxurious conditions, as we learn when Pharaoh orders,
" . . . settle your father and your brothers in the best part of
the land" (Gen. 47, 6). In fact, Joseph gave them much more: he
made them proprietors of the prime land: "So Joseph settled
his father and his brothers, giving them holdings (אחזה) in the
choicest part of the land of Egypt, in the region of Rameses, as
Pharaoh has commanded" (vs. 11). Joseph even supplies all
his brothers' food so that they would not need to worry about
hunger: "Joseph sustained his father and his brothers and all
his father's household with bread, down to the little ones"
(vs. 12).

27 See Daube (n. 5), pp. 62-72; see below pp. 46-47.
28 Daube, pp. 73-78; see below pp. 52-53.

The conditions in which the Israelites live stand in stark contrast to those of the Egyptians. Verses 13-26 bear testimony that the Egyptians and their land were subjugated to Pharaoh for the bread they received to keep themselves alive. The Israelites settled "in the choicest part of the land" and were sustained "with bread," while about the Egyptians we hear: "Now there was no bread in the land, for the famine was very severe" (vs. 13). The verses which immediately follow describe the deterioration in their economic situation. At first, Joseph "gathers in all the money that was to be found in the land of Egypt . . . " (vs. 14) as payment for bread. Then, when there is no money anymore, the desperate Egyptians beg: "Give us bread, *lest we die* before your very eyes" (vs. 15), an appeal reminding us of the complaint voiced by the children of Israel in the desert: "*If only we had died* by the hand of the Lord in the land of Egypt, when we sat by the fleshpots, when we ate our fill of bread, for you have brought us out into this wilderness to starve this whole congregation to death" (Ex. 16, 3; cf. Nu. 11, 5; 16, 13). In the desert, Israel pays for their having been favored in Egypt.

Joseph takes advantage of the Egyptians' hunger and exchanges their livestock for bread (vs. 16). Those stores last for one year only (vs. 17), at the end of which the Egyptians, with nothing more to trade for bread, offer themselves and their land to Joseph as barter: " . . . nothing is left at my lord's disposal save our persons and our farmland. Let us not perish before your eyes, both we and our land. Take us and our land in exchange for bread, and we with our land *will be slaves to Pharaoh*" (vss. 18-19). These last words are echoed in Deuteronomy 6, 21: "*We were slaves to Pharaoh* in Egypt," suggesting a causal relationship.

Joseph follows the Egyptians' advice: "So Joseph gained possession of all the land of Egypt for Pharaoh, every Egyptian having sold his field because *the famine was severe* for them . . . " (vs. 20). The last words in this verse recall the language of Genesis 41, 56-57: "Accordingly, when *the famine became severe* in the land of Egypt, Joseph laid open all that was within, and rationed out grain to the Egyptians. The famine, however, spread over the whole land. So all the land came to Joseph in Egypt to procure rations, for *the famine had become severe* throughout the land." The resemblance, however, only emphasizes the tension between the two: according to 41, 56, the Egyptians do not have to pay for grain during the years of famine. The notion that grain was given to them for free corresponds with their not being paid for the grain they gave to Pharaoh in the years of plenty: "Let all the food of these good years that are coming be gathered, and let the grain be collected under Pharaoh's authority as food be stored in the cities. Let that food be a reserve for the land for the seven years of famine which will come upon the land of Egypt, so that the land may not perish in the famine . . . And he gathered all the grain of the seven years that the land of Egypt was enjoying and stored the grain in the cities . . . " (vss. 35-36, 48). In the years of famine, Pharaoh merely returns to the Egyptians what he took from them during the seven good years.

Thus, it seems to me that verses 12-26 make up a secondary element in the Joseph narrative. The tendency of these verses is to put Joseph to blame for maltreating the Egyptians. They make his deeds appear even more malevolent by portraying Joseph as selling to the Egyptians what he had received freely from them beforehand.

Additional proof of the secondary status of verses 12-26 is the repetitive resumption of verse 27, which follows the interpolation and repeats verse 11 (we will discuss this in a moment).[29] The description of the Egyptians' struggle in the famine severs the natural continuity of verses 11 and 28 which deal with Jacob and his sons.

29 For examples of this literary phenomenon, see C. Kuhl, "Die Wiederaufnahme, ein literarkritisches Prinzip?" *ZAW* 64 (1952), pp. 1-11.

Why Were the Israelites Enslaved in Egypt?

The Egyptians' desperate offer to Joseph opens with a reference to their land and ends with a reference to their own des-
tiny. In Joseph's acceptance, the land comes first and the Egyptians follow. In the MT of verse 21 we read: ואת העם העביר אותם
לערים = "And the people, he moved them to the cities," but the
version of the Samaritan Pentateuch and the Septuagint
should be preferred: ואת העם העביד אותם לעבדים = "And the people, he enslaved them as slaves," since there is no logic in the
people's transfer: in the subsequent verses it becomes clear they
continue to cultivate their own land (vs. 23). In my opinion, the
MT version is not the product of a scribal error (the change of a
ד into a ר [העביר ← העביד, and לעבדים ← לערים] followed by the
omission of a letter [the ב in לעבדים]), but expresses a scribe's
purposeful reading. In order to avoid an overt statement that
Joseph caused the enslavement of the Egyptians, that scribe
subverted the main point of the story, the 'measure for measure' explanation for the Israelites' servitude in Egypt.[30]

Joseph is sensitive enough not to use derivations of the root
עב"ד (= "to serve") when he assures the Egyptians that he has
accepted their proposal: "Whereas I have this day acquired
you and your land for Pharaoh . . . " (vs. 23). The Egyptians
themselves are the ones who overtly mention their enslavement once again: "We are grateful to my lord, and we shall be
servants to Pharaoh" (vs. 25).

Not all the Egyptians are subjugated to Pharaoh: "Only the
land of the priests he did not take over, for the priests had an
allotment from Pharaoh, and they lived off the allotment
which Pharaoh had made to them; therefore they did not sell

---

30 A similar polemical tendency is expressed in Josephus Flavius'
retelling of this episode. At first he claims that the Egyptians
suffered from the famine because "nor did they indeed make the
least provision for themselves, so ignorant were they what was
to be done," and he proceeds to recount that Joseph returned their
fields to them: ". . . and gave them back entirely the land
which, by their own consent, the king might have possessed
alone . . . " (*Ant.* 2, 7, 7).

41

their land" (vs. 22). Another verse in the story supports this statement: "And Joseph made it a law in Egypt, which is still valid . . . only the land of the priests did not become Pharaoh's" (vs. 26).

I do not discount the possibility that these two verses represent a secondary stratum of the story—like many other etiological elements in the biblical narrative[31]—a stratum added to the story in order to give it a touch of authenticity. Verse 22 indeed interrupts the natural continuity between the subjugation of the Egyptian people (vs. 21) and Joseph's words to them, which grant validity to the deal, and in any case verse 26 stands at the end of the story. Whether or not these verses are secondary, they fit Joseph's policy of favoring his relatives: Joseph's wife is a priest's daughter: " . . . and he gave him for a wife Asenath daughter of Potiphera, priest of On" (41, 45; see also vss. 50 and 46, 20). Verse 27, which follows the end of the Egyptians' discrimination story, is, as mentioned above, a repetitive resumption that returns us to Jacob and his house:

vs. 11	*vs. 27*
So Joseph settled his father and his brothers, giving them *holdings* in the choicest part of *the land of Egypt,* in *the land of Rameses,*	Thus Israel settled in *the land of Egypt,* in *the land of Goshen* and *they acquired holdings in it,* and were fertile and increased greatly.

31 See I. L. Seeligmann, "Etiological Elements in Biblical Historiography," *Zion* 26 (1961), pp. 151-157 (Hebrew). The word "only" (vs. 22) also seems to testify to the secondary nature of this element, see for instance 1 Kings 15, 5, 23.

as Pharaoh had
commanded.

The subjugation of the Egyptians and their land is total. The
end of the story emphasizes that the Israelites own property
in Egypt: "And they acquired holdings in it."

The different names designating the Israelite territory also
deserve our attention: "the land of Goshen" (vs. 27) is the common name (see for instance vss. 4, 6), while "the land of
Rameses" (vs. 11) reappears only in a secondary element of the
Joseph narrative in the Septuagint of 46, 28. In other verses,
Rameses is the name of a city (Ex. 1, 11; 12, 37; Nu. 33, 5). According to Exodus 1, 11, Rameses was one of the store cities built
by the Israelite slaves to Pharaoh: " . . . and they built store
cities for Pharaoh: Pithom and Rameses." It is not impossible
that the name of the land in Genesis 47, 11—Rameses—hints
at a 'measure for measure' punishment: because they sat peace-
fully in the land of Rameses while all the Egyptians suffered
from hunger, enslaved to Pharaoh, they will become the king's
slaves and build the city of Rameses. Moreover, Rameses is a
store city:[32] the Israelites, who enjoyed a free supply of food
from the Egyptians' bumper crop which was taken from them
and stored by Joseph during the seven fertile years (41, 47),
will suffer now building cities to warehouse food for Pharaoh.

The Septuagint (or its Hebrew *Vorlage*) may have taken
note of the interrelationship between our story and the building of the store cities in Exodus 1, 11. It adds a third city to the
list of store-cities the enslaved Israelites built—"On, which is
Heliopolis." The name reminds us of Joseph's father-in-law,

---

32 This meaning of the term becomes clear from 2 Chronicles 32, 28:
"And store cities for the produce of grain, wine and oil . . . "; see
for instance Targum Onqeles to Exodus 1, 11: קרוי בית אוצרא. The
term is related to the Akkadian word maškānati (store, house,
barn); see B. Mazar, *Biblical Encyclopaedia* 5, pp. 165-167
(Hebrew).

"the priest of On" who, like the other priests, was not enslaved by Joseph to Pharaoh, as mentioned above.

Verse 27 has an extra element which has no parallel in verse 11: "and *were fertile* and *increased greatly,*" words which makes it clear the Israelites suffered no hunger or shortage during the seven bad years. These words are echoed in the story of the Israelite enslavement in Exodus 1, 7: "But the Israelites *were fertile* and prolific; they multiplied and *increased very greatly,* so that the land was filled with them." Their proliferation during the years of famine is the cause of their enslavement.

The Egyptian enslavement story emphasizes that everything Joseph does is for the benefit of Pharaoh: "And Joseph brought the money into *Pharaoh's* palace" (47, 15); "and we with our land will be slaves to *Pharaoh*" (vs. 19); "So Joseph gained possession of all the farmland of Egypt *for Pharaoh* . . . thus the land passed over *to Pharaoh*" (vs. 20); "Whereas I have this day acquired you and your land *for Pharaoh*" (vs. 23); "and we shall be slaves *to Pharaoh*" (vs. 25). But all of Joseph's attempts to satisfy his master cannot help the Israelites when a "new king arose over Egypt who did not know Joseph" (Ex. 1, 8): a king who fears the Israelites' proliferation (vss. 9-11).

I

I have tried to show that the lack of any overt reasons in the Bible explaining the cause of the Israelite enslavement in Egypt by no means implies that biblical literature had no interest in the question; the book of Genesis conceals a number of covert answers sharing a single spirit: a 'measure for measure' punishment. Abraham sinned by leaving Canaan for Egypt and by abandoning his wife in order to save his own life; Sarah and Abraham sinned in their treatment of Hagar, the Egyptian maidservant and her son Ishmael; Joseph's brothers sinned by casting him into the pit and by selling him to Egypt; Joseph himself sinned by enslaving the Egyptians and favoring his own brothers. The understanding of the Israelites' enslavement as a punishment finds other expressions as well, such as the reference to the Egyptian bondage as "the iron blast furnace," and the presentation of the imminent return to Egypt as a punishment. The punishment motif is apparent as well in the portrayal of other captivity scenes in which the punishment element is made overt and which are consistent with the Exodus literary pattern, such as Jacob in Haran and the Ark in the land of the Philistines, examples we will discuss further in the next chapter.

CHAPTER TWO

The Many Covert Faces of the
Exodus Pattern

A

The Exodus, the central event in the historiography of the Bible and in the collective memory of the biblical period, represents an historical watershed. It shapes the recounting of events both before and after it: at the dawn of history and the time of the patriarchs, as well as events and periods long after the Exodus itself. The majority of these events, early and late, carry the literary mark of the Exodus discreetly: their resemblance to the Exodus is not mentioned outright, leaving it to the reader to decipher the hints and uncover the implicit links.[1]

Among the earliest events cloaked in the Exodus pattern are the story of Abraham and Sarah in Egypt (Gen. 12, 10-20), discussed in detail in the first chapter,[2] and Jacob's journey to Haran, his enslavement to Laban and his departure from there with great wealth (Gen. 29-31). The Passover Haggadah already makes the unflattering comparison between Laban and Pharaoh:[3] "Come and learn what Laban the Aramean

1   For overt references to the Exodus see Y. Hoffmann, *The Doctrine of the Exodus in the Bible*, Tel-Aviv 1983 (Hebrew).
2   See pp. 18-26 and also pp. 55-56.
3   Of course, the Haggadah has its own agenda here in wishing to portray Laban as more evil than Pharoah. What's more, the comparison made in the Haggadah is based on an incorrect

46

tried to do to Jacob our father! For Pharaoh decreed the death of the male children only, but Laban tried to destroy us all—as it is said: 'An Aramean sought to destroy my father . . . ' "(Dt. 26, 5). Let us consider the similarities between these two narratives in the Bible:[4]

a. In both stories, the Hebrews are warmly welcomed by their hosts (both stories deal with Jacob and his house).

b. The Hebrews serve their hosts with hard labor.

c. The children of Jacob multiply both in Padan Aram and in Egypt (the root פר"ץ [to spread out] is used for the flocks in Gen. 30, 43 and for humans in Ex. 1, 12).

d. The host tries to deter proliferation (of flocks in Genesis and of humans in Exodus).

e. God sees the burden of the Hebrews and wants them to return to their country (compare Gen. 31, 12-13 with Ex. 3, 6-8).

f. The Hebrews request their own release (Gen. 30, 25; Ex. 7, 16; and other instances).

g. Both stories record a departure with great wealth (expressed with the root נצ"ל [to take away, strip]: Gen. 31, 9; Ex. 3, 22).

h. The Hebrews escape (Gen. 31, 20; Ex. 14, 5).

i. In both stories the host is informed of the escape, using the very same language: " . . . was told that . . . had fled" (Gen. 31, 22; Ex. 14, 5).

j. The oppressor pursues the Hebrews (Gen. 31, 23; Ex. 14, 7-8).

k. Laban overtakes Jacob (Gen. 31, 25) and Pharaoh expresses his wish to overtake the Hebrews (Ex. 15, 9).

l. God interferes with the pursuer—He warns Laban (Gen. 31, 24) and causes the Egyptians to drown (Ex. 14-15).

understanding of the term ארמי אבד, which is a "fugitive Aramean."

4   See D. Daube, *The Exodus Pattern in the Bible*, London 1983, pp. 62-72.

The close kinship between the Jacob narrative and the Exodus encourages us to perceive both the story of Abraham's descent to Egypt and the story of Jacob's journey to his fathers' homeland as part of a carefully planned geographical-historical scheme: Abraham leaves Mesopotamia (Haran) and comes to Canaan (Gen. 12, 4-5), then descends further to Egypt because of famine and eventually returns to Canaan (12, 10-20). His son Isaac, the second patriarch, is born in Canaan and does not leave the country despite the famine (see the divine prohibition to go down to Egypt [26, 2]); Jacob first goes to Mesopotamia (Haran, 28, 10), returns to Canaan (33, 18) and then, driven by famine, descends with his entire family to Egypt in the wake of his son Joseph (ch. 46), having received divine permission to leave the country and the promise they will return (vss. 3-4).

The descent of Jacob and his children is not the end of the process: after their return to Canaan and their long, tumultuous history in the land, they are punished with exile in Mesopotamia, the close of the continuous historical narrative extending from "When God began to create" (Gen. 1, 1) to the report of the exiled king of Judah, Jehoiachin: " . . . his prison garments were removed . . . regular allotment of food was given him at the instance of the king . . . all the days of his life" (2 Ki. 25, 30). This, then, is the complete geographical scheme, the "W" pattern:

Haran		Haran		Mesopotamia
Canaan	Canaan	Canaan		Canaan
	Egypt		Egypt	

Among the post-Exodus periods, the influence of the pattern can be easily traced in the formation of the judges era. The Exodus is overtly mentioned in the book of Judges, for example, in the words of Gideon, who is aware of the past salvation, and wonders why God does not intervene once again with His awesome power:[5] "Gideon said to him, 'Please, my lord, if the Lord is with us, why has all this befallen us? Where are all his wondrous deeds about which our fathers told us, saying "Truly the Lord brought us up from Egypt"? Now the Lord has abandoned us and delivered us into the hands of Midian' " (6, 13). It seems to me that Gideon's question, which remained unanswered, motivated the addition of an anomalous element in the book: the appearance of a prophet, a Moses-like figure (6, 7-10), who opens his speech with the declaration, "I brought you up out of Egypt and freed you from the house of bondage. I rescued you from the Egyptians and from all your oppressors . . . " (vss. 8-9). Verses 7-10 are indeed missing from a copy of the book of Judges found in Qumran.[6] A further proof for the secondary nature of verses 7-10 is the fact that the beginning of the interpolation is a related expansion:[7] verse 7 repeats verse 6: " And the Israelites cried out to the Lord" (v. 6); "When the Israelites cried to the Lord" (vs. 7). The addition explains why the Israelites are not saved by God and why the Exodus miracles are not repeated at the present time: because of Israel's sins. The interpolation also clarifies the nature of the sins mentioned in verse 1: "And I said to you . . . 'You must not worship the gods of the Amorites in whose land you dwell.' But you did not obey Me" (vs. 10).

As in the prophet's speech, the angel's words at the beginning of the book of Judges recall God's favor, the Exodus, in contrast to the sin of idolatry: "I brought you up from Egypt and I took you into the land which I had promised on oath to your fathers . . . And you, for your part, must make no covenant with the inhabitants of this land; you must tear down their

---

5   On relationships between the Gideon cycle and the Exodus, see below, pp. 67-69.

6   R. G. Boling, *Judges (AB)*, Garden City, New York 1975, p. 40.

7   A. Rofé, *The Book of Balaam (Numbers 22, 2-24, 25)*, Jerusalem 1979, p. 56 (Hebrew) .

altars. But you have not obeyed Me—look what you have done!" (2, 1-2; cf. 6, 10). The tension between God's favors and Israel's sin is also expressed in the programmatic and deuteronomistic introduction to the book of Judges: "[the Is-raelites] . . . forsook the Lord, the God of their fathers, who had brought them out of the land of Egypt. They followed other gods . . . " (2, 12-13; see also 10, 13).[8] The terms used in this introduction to describe Israel's suffering are borrowed from the dictionary of the Egyptian bondage. Compare: "for the Lord would be moved to pity by *their moanings* because of *those who oppressed* and crushed them" (2, 18) to Exodus 2, 24: "God heard *their moaning*"; 6, 5: "I have now heard the *moan-ing* of the Israelites . . . "; 3, 9: " . . . I have seen how the Egyptians *oppress* them" (this term appears in the book of Judges in other verses as well: 1, 34; 4, 3; 6, 9; 10, 12).

Texts in which God tries Israel in the wilderness and which are accompanied by accounts of punishments[9] also find their parallel in the period of the Judges: "I for My part will no longer drive out before them any of the nations that Joshua left when he died. For it was in order to test Israel by them— [to see] whether or not they would walk faithfully in the ways of the Lord, as their fathers had done . . . " (2, 21-22); "These served as a means of testing Israel, to learn whether they would obey the commandments which the Lord had en-joined upon their fathers through Moses" (3, 4).[10]

Some additional acts of salvation in the book of Judges are painted with the colors of the Exodus. In the prose version of Deborah and Barak's victory over the Canaanites, we read: "And I will draw Sisera . . . with his chariots and his troops, toward you up to the Wadi Kishon; and I will deliver him

8   For more overt references to the Exodus in the book of Judges, see 11, 13, 16; 19, 30.
9   See pp. 109-111.
10   For a different concept of the test through which God tries Israel in that period, see 3, 1.

into your hands" (4, 7); "And the Lord threw Sisera and all his chariots and army into a panic before the onslaught of Barak" (vs. 15). This victory reminds us of the Egyptians' defeat at the Sea of Reeds, where we read: "At the morning watch, the Lord looked down upon the Egyptian army from a pillar of fire and cloud, and threw the Egyptian army into a panic" (Ex. 14, 24). The poetic version, that of the Song of Deborah, emphasizes the miraculous nature of the Canaanite defeat in a manner resembling the Egyptian fall: "The stars fought from heaven, From their courses they fought against Sisera. The torrent Kishon swept them away, The raging torrent, the torrent Kishon" (5, 20-21). The Song of Deborah also mentions Mount Sinai in an overt association with the Exodus traditions: "The mountains quaked—Before the Lord, Him of Sinai, Before the Lord, God of Israel" (vs. 5). The scene of a woman, a prophetess (4, 4), singing with the male savior and praising God for the victory described in the previous chapter—"On that day Deborah and Barak son of Abinoam sang . . . " (5, 1)—follows the well-known pattern of Exodus 14-15: "Then Miriam the prophetess . . . took a timbrel in her hand, and all the women went out after her in dance with timbrels. And Miriam chanted for them: Sing to the Lord, for He has triumphed gloriously; Horse and driver He has hurled into the sea" (15, 20-21); Miriam's words are a literal repetition of the beginning of the song of Moses: "I will sing to the Lord, for He has triumphed gloriously; Horse and driver He has hurled into the sea . . . " (vs. 1).

The journey of the tribe of Dan northwards, and their settlement in the city of Dan (Jud. 17-18), also follow the Exodus and conquest patterns, as Malamat has shown.[11] He enumerates ten points in which this story follows the pattern:

11 A. Malamat, "The Danite Migration and the Pan-Israelite Exodus-Conquest: Biblical Narrative Pattern," *Biblica* 51 (1970), pp. 1-16.

1. direct association with Moses or his descendents (see Jud. 18, 30, where the original reading is Moses [משה] and not Manasseh [מנשה]);[12]

2. the dispatch of spies selected from the tribal notables and the gathering of intelligence;

3. the report of the spies;

4. misgivings of the people in reaction to the spies' report (see: "And you are sitting idle" [Jud. 18, 9]);

5. the mention of the non-combatants and cattle accompanying the warriors (see 18, 21);

6. the particular number of armed warriors as "six hundred" (18, 11; cf. Ex. 12, 37-38);

7. oracular consultation, by a levite priest, concerning the course of the campaign;

8. the procurement of cultic objects in transit, and their eventual deposition at the final destination of the campaign;

9. permanence of priesthood secured by a third-generation priest (Jud. 18, 30; cf. Nu. 25);

10. renaming of places conquered and resettled by the Israelites (Jud. 18, 29; cf. for instance Jud. 1, 10-11, 17, 23).

Another example of an event subsequent to the Exodus which was molded in its pattern is the series of adventures of the Ark of God in the land of the Philistines, the plagues with which the capturers are smitten, and its safe return to its own country, in 1 Samuel 5, 1-6, 18. The interrelationship between the Samuel and Exodus narratives is an overt one, as testified by the Philistines' words when the Ark of God reaches the camp: "Woe to us! Who will save us from the power of this mighty God? He is the same God who struck the Egyptians with every kind of plague in the wilderness!" (1 Sam. 4, 8). The link is suggested once again in the words of the Philistine priests,

---

12 Thus in some Greek manuscripts and in the Vulgate. Rabbinic literature provides reasons for the change from Moses to Mannasseh (see BT *Berakhot* 9a; *Baba Bathra* 109b).

who instruct their people to send the Ark back to its place: "Do not harden your hearts as the Egyptians and Pharaoh hardened their hearts. As you know, when he made mockery of them, they had to let Israel go and they departed" (6, 6).

Additional covert resemblances between the two stories exist. Both stories deal with an entity in exile (Israel, the Ark) which is prevented from returning to Canaan; and only plagues of disease and death convince the capturers to free their captives. The plague is not limited to humans but harms the capturers' gods as well: the etiological narrative[13] about Dagon's fall before the Ark may be a secondary element in the story (see the resumptive repetition in 5, 1-2),[14] which serves to assimilate the Ark story to the Exodus pattern: " . . . and I will mete out punishments to all the gods of Egypt" (Ex. 12, 12; see also Nu. 33, 4). In both stories the leaders are asked by their people to set the captives free (Ex. 10, 7; 1 Sam. 5, 11) and the captives leave with great wealth (Ex. 3, 22; 12, 35 [see also Gen. 15, 14]; 1 Sam. 6, 4-11). The two stories share the same vocabulary: striking (הכ"ה; see for example Ex. 8, 13; 9, 25; 1 Sam. 5, 6, 9, 12); plague (נג"ף; see for example Ex. 7, 27; 9, 14; 1 Sam. 6, 4); territory (גבול; Ex. 7, 27; 10, 14, 19; 1 Sam. 5, 6); healing (רפ"א; Ex. 15, 26; 1 Sam. 6, 3).[15]

Similarities to the Exodus narrative are not limited to the historiographical composition of Genesis-Kings. The resemblances between the book of Esther and the Joseph cycle—the foundation of the Exodus narrative—are well known,[16] but

---

13 Actually, this is a pseudo-etiological narrative—a story shaped like an etiological narrative, but tendentious and even polemical. (More examples of such pseudo-etiological narratives are Gen. 19, 30-38 and Jud. 15, 18-19.)

14 The term is borrowed, as mentioned above, from Rofé (see n. 7), p. 56.

15 Read also Daube (see n. 4), pp. 72-88.

16 L. A. Rosenthal, "Die Josephgeschichte mit den Büchern Ester und Daniel verglichen," ZAW 15 (1895), pp. 278-284; idem,

many threads tie the scroll to the bondage and redemption story itself:

a. Moses, the savior of Israel, grows up in the royal palace, while Esther is also taken into the home of the king.

b. Fear is invoked by the children of Israel (Ex. 1, 9; Est. 3, 8). There is a desire to annihilate them (Ex. 1, 16, 22; Est. 3, 9). An allusion to the servitude of the Israelites in Egypt, and their enslavement before Pharaoh decided to kill the male infants, is put into Esther's mouth: " . . . Had we only been sold as bondmen and bondwomen I would have kept silent . . . " (7, 4).

c. The ten plagues in Egypt, climaxed by the plague of the first-born, find their counterpart in the killing of Haman's ten sons (Est. 9, 7-10).

d. The Israelites' enemies meet their death in the sea, while, in the scroll, the Jews kill their enemies (Ex. 14, 26-28; Est. 9, 5-6; 15).

e. The unpleasant aspect of the despoiling of the Egyptians (Ex. 3, 22) may have motivated the statement that the Jews "did not lay hands on the spoil" (Est. 9, 10, 15, 16).

f. During the Exodus, the Israelites fight with the Amalekites, who become a symbol of Israel's enemies. Israel is commanded to take revenge on the Amalekites in the future (Ex. 17, 14-16; Dt. 25, 17-19). Saul and his house did not do their duty (1 Sam. 15) and the unfinished matter is brought up again in the book of Esther. Mordecai is a descendant of Saul: "In the fortress Shushan lived a Jew by the name of Mordecai, son of Jair son of Shimei son of Kish, a Benjaminite" (2, 5),[17]

"Nochmals der Vergleich Ester, Joseph-Daniel," *ZAW* 17 (1897), pp. 125-128; M. Gan, "The Book of Esther in the Light of the Story of Joseph in Egypt," *Tarbiz* 31 (1962), pp. 144-149 (Hebrew).

17   Not only the name Kish testifies for Saul's family, but the name Shimei as well (2 Sam. 16, 5). Moreover, the House of Saul and the tribe of Benjamin have close relations with the people of Gilead (see Jud. 21, 5-14) and Jair is indeed a Gileadite name (see

while Haman is an "Agagite" (3, 1), a descendent of King Agag, Saul's enemy. Only here, in the book of Esther, is the historical account finally paid.

But as much as the Esther narrative resembles the Exodus narrative, it has even more elements in common with another Exodus-like story, that of Abraham and Sarah in Egypt (Gen. 12, 10-20):

a. Both stories tell of a Hebrew/Jew in exile (Gen. 12, 10; Est. 2, 5-6).

b. A male figure is accompanied by his female relative (Gen. 12, 11; Est. 2, 7).

c. Both women are beautiful (Gen. 12, 11; Est. 2, 7).

d. Both women are taken to the royal palace: "And the woman was taken into Pharaoh's palace" (Gen. 12, 15); "Esther was taken to King Ahasuerus in his royal palace" (Est. 2, 16).

e. The woman hides her true identity in obedience to her male relative: "Please say that you are my sister" (Gen. 12, 13); "Esther did not reveal her people as her kindred, for Mordecai had told her not to reveal it" (Est. 2, 10; see also vs. 20).

f. The woman is taken to be the king's wife: " . . . so that I took her to be my wife" (Gen. 12, 19); "So he set a royal diadem on her head and made her queen instead of Vashti" (Est. 2, 17).

g. In both books the life of the Hebrews/Jews (especially the woman's relatives) are threatened: " . . . they will kill me and let you live" (Gen. 12, 12); " . . . Haman plotted to do away with all the Jews, Mordecai's people" (Est. 3, 6; see also vs. 13).

h. The man hopes to save himself or his people by virtue of the woman: " . . . that I may remain alive thanks to you"

for instance Jud. 10, 3-5), as is Abihail (Est. 2, 15), the name of a Gadite family closely related to the Gilead (1 Chr. 5, 14).

55

(Gen. 12, 13); " . . . and charge her to go to the king and to appeal to him and to plead with him for her people" (Est. 4, 8).

i. The king discovers the true relation between the man and the woman: "Pharoah sent for Abram and said, 'What is this you have done to me! Why did you not tell me she was your wife?' " (Gen. 12, 18); "Mordecai presented himself to the king, for Esther had revealed how he was related to her" (Est. 8, 1).

j. The enemies are punished: "But the Lord afflicted Pharaoh and his household with mighty plagues" (Gen. 12, 17); "The king has permitted the Jews . . . to destroy, massacre and exterminate . . . " (Est. 8, 11; see also 9, 5-15).

k. The Hebrews benefit from the conflict: "And because of her, it went well with Abram; he acquired sheep, oxen, asses, male and female slaves, she-asses and camels" (Gen. 12, 16); " . . . and plunder their possessions" (Est. 8, 11).

Post-biblical sources reinforce the relationship between the two stories. The Genesis Apocryphon, for example, tells that Pharaoh gave Abraham "many garments of fine linen and purple" (לבוש די בוץ וארגואן; pl. XX lines 31-32), following Esther 8, 15: "Mordecai left the king's presence in royal robes of blue and white" (בוץ וארגמן; 8, 15). A midrashic fragment from the Cairo Geniza (*Geniza Studies in Memory of S. Schecter* by L. Ginzberg, New York 1928, p. 19) draws an analogy between the permission granted Esther to enter the king's bed and that granted Sarah to be with the Egyptian king; in both cases the threat to human life outweighed the danger of conducting forbidden relations.[18]

All the raw materials needed to construct scenarios of the future redemption are found in the traditions of the past

18   See J. Finkel, "The Author of the Genesis Apocryphon Knew the Book of Esther," *Essays on the Dead Sea Scrolls (in memory of E.L. Sukenik)*, edited by C. Rabin and Y. Yadin, Jerusalem 1961, pp. 163-182.

redemption, the Exodus, sometimes amalgamated with elements borrowed from Creation traditions (Isa. 11, 15-16; 51, 9-10).[19] The prophet Micah makes the equation overt: "I will show him wondrous deeds as in the days when you sallied forth from the land of Egypt" (7, 15). The prophecy of Deutero-Isaiah is replete with redemption descriptions reminiscent of the Exodus; some discernable elements include: the departure itself (48, 20; 52, 11-12); the parting of the sea (42, 15; 43, 2, 16-18; 44, 27; 50, 2-3; 51, 10-11) and the supply of water to the thirsty ones in the wilderness (41, 17-18; 43, 19-20; 48, 21; 49, 10-11 [including the supply of food]).[20]

The Exodus was the event that created the relationship between God and His people in the past (see for instance: "They never asked themselves, 'Where is the Lord, who brought us up from the land of Egypt . . . ' " [Jer. 2, 6]), but the foreseen redemption from Babylon takes the place of the Exodus: "Assuredly, a time is coming—declares the Lord—when it shall no more be said, 'As the Lord lives who brought the Israelites out of the land of Egypt'; but rather, 'As the Lord lives who brought the Israelites out of the northland, and out of all the lands to which he had banished them.' For I will bring them back to their land which I gave to their fathers" (Jer. 16, 14-15).

The historiography of the redemption is also influenced by the Exodus pattern, as becomes clear from the declaration of Cyrus of Persia: " . . . and whoever stays behind, wherever he may be living (אשר הוא גר שם), let the people of his place assist him with *silver, gold,* goods and livestock, besides the freewill offering to the house of God that is in Jerusalem" (Ezr. 1, 4). The realization of the command, "all their *neighbors* supported them with *silver vessels,* with *gold,* with *goods* (ברכוש), with livestock and with precious objects . . . " (vs. 6), recalls the well-known motif of the Exodus: "Each woman

19   See below, p. 103.
20   See Hoffmann (n. 1), especially p. 61.

shall borrow from her *neighbor* and the lodger of her house *objects of silver and gold,* and clothing . . . " (Ex. 3, 22; see also 12, 35). The word רכוש (goods, wealth) appears in the Exodus context in the promise to Abraham about the future return of his sons to Canaan: "and in the end they shall go free with great wealth" (רכוש גדול; Gen. 15, 14). Livestock is mentioned in Exodus 12, 38, and also in the description of Abraham's return from Egypt: "Now Abram was very rich in *cattle, silver and gold"* (Gen. 13, 2).

Before we conclude this review of periods and events which were modelled after the Exodus, let us consider the relationship between an Exodus-like story and some biblical laws. For instance, there is a command to give the released Hebrew slave some goods because of the Exodus: "Bear in mind that you were slaves in the land of Egypt and the Lord your God redeemed you; therefore I enjoin this commandment upon you today" (Dt. 15, 15). The injunction continues: "When you do set him free, do not feel aggrieved, for double the service of a hired servant he has served you, six years" (vs. 18). The words "six years" are equal to "double the service of a hired servant"; since משנה indeed means "double" (Ex. 16, 22; Job 42, 10), "the service of a hired servant" refers to a fixed time of service of three years.

This contention of a three year period of servitude is verified by Isaiah 16, 14: "And now the Lord has spoken: in three years, like the years of a hired servant, the glory of Moab will be brought into contempt." Yet it seems to be contradicted by another verse in Isaiah: "For thus my Lord has said to me: in another year like the years of a hired servant, all the glory of Kedar will come to an end" (21, 16). In contrast to the Masoretic text, however, the version of the complete Isaiah scroll from Qumran reads: "In three years, according to the years of a hired servant . . . ," thereby confirming the assumption that three years is the fixed time of service. It appears that the version in the Isaiah scroll is preferable because it gives meaning to the plural form "according to the years."

The word שכיר ("a hired servant"), in Deuteronomy 15, 18 and in the above-quoted verses from Isaiah, seems to refer to a distinct type of slavery. Indeed, a literary parallelism in Job 7, 1-2 bears witness that the שכיר is a certain kind of slave: "The man has a term of service on earth; his days are like those of a hired servant (שכיר)—like a slave (עבד) who longs for [evening's] shadows, like a hired servant (שכיר) who waits for his wage." In fact, an extra-biblical source, namely the Laws of Hammurabi (§117) specifies a three-year period of servitude for debt and release in the fourth: "If a man has become liable to arrest under a bond and has sold his wife, his son or his daughter or gives [them] into servitude, for three years they shall do work in the house of him who has bought them or taken them into servitude, in the fourth year their release shall be granted."[21] In the biblical law of the Hebrew slave, the three-year period of servitude was apparently replaced with a six-year period because of the wish to link the number of years of servitude and release to two other significant units of time: the number of workdays in the week and the Sabbath, and the number of years of agricultural work and the sabbatical year.[22]

The law was altered, but an imprint of the old law can still be detected in the story of the covenant between the pieces (Gen. 15), in which every year of slavery becomes a generation in the life of the oppressed Israelite nation; God promises Abraham that "They shall return here in the fourth

21   The translation of the law is according to G. R. Driver and J. C. Miles, *The Babylonian Laws*, Oxford 1955, vol. 2, pp. 47-49.

22   Indeed, in Deuteronomy we find the law of servitude (15, 12-18) adjacent to the law of the sabbatical year (15, 1-11). See also Jeremiah 34, which is influenced by Deuteronomy 15 and, in citing the law of servitude (Jer. 34, 14), borrows an idiom from the law of the sabbatical year: "At the end of every seven years" (Dt. 15, 1).

generation" (vs. 16), after three generations of servitude. In the visual section of the story one can also perceive the contrast between the third and the fourth. The number "three" is mentioned three times in this section: "Bring me a three-year-old heifer, a three-year-old she-goat, a three-year old ram" (vs. 9). In contrast to these three, which are dismembered, the two birds, "a turtledove and a young bird" (ibid.), or in their collective designation "the bird" (vs. 10), are not cut apart. The three dismembered animals symbolize the three enslaved generations in Egypt while the birds that remain whole symbolize the fourth generation, which is released and returns to its land.

In the same chapter, the presentation of God as "a smoking oven and a flaming torch" (vs. 17) foretells the manner in which God will go before the children of Israel in the wilderness "in a pillar of cloud by day . . . and in a pillar of fire by night . . . " (Ex. 13, 21). Moreover, the passing of God "between those pieces" (בין הגזרים האלה; vs. 17), using the term גזרים rather than בתרים (see vs. 10 and also Jer. 34, 19), is paralleled by the parting of the Sea of Reeds: "Who split apart the Sea of Reeds (לגזר ים סוף לגזרים) . . . and made Israel to pass through it" (Ps. 136, 13-14).

B

Another aspect we must examine in our search for stories modelled after the Exodus are those biblical characters formed in the image of Moses, the hero of the Exodus. Many stories about Joshua, Gideon, Elijah and Elisha are reflections of parallel stories about Moses, although the circles in which they were created and the contexts into which they were incorporated necessitated a very different presentation. The process of assimilating characters to Moses did not end with the canonization of the Hebrew Bible. It is well known, for instance, that Jesus is in many ways a second Moses. Here, however, we will discuss only biblical characters, presenting a few examples to illustrate each figure.

It comes as no surprise that Joshua, Moses' disciple and successor, is fashioned in the image of his master (see Ex. 17, 13-14; 32, 17; 33, 11; Nu. 11, 28; 27, 18-23; Dt. 31, 14-23). The first words of the book of Joshua read: "After the death of Moses the servant of the Lord, the Lord said to Joshua son of Nun, Moses' attendant: 'My servant Moses is dead. Prepare to cross the Jordan, together with all this people ... No one shall be able to resist you as long as you live. As I was with Moses, so I will be with you: I will not fail you or forsake you' " (1, 1-5).

We have already mentioned that the Exodus, which began with the parting of the Sea of Reeds, ends with the parting of the Jordan and the entrance into Canaan in the book of Joshua.[23] Many prominent resemblances indeed link the two narratives.[24] Let us focus, however, on a single major difference: In the story of the Sea of Reeds, Moses wields an instrument: "And you lift up your rod and hold out your arm over the sea and split it ... " (Ex. 14, 16). In the parallel story, the priests who bear the Ark of the Lord work wonders: "When the feet of the priests bearing the Ark of the Lord, the Sovereign of all the earth, come to rest in the waters of the Jordan, the waters of the Jordan ... will be cut off and will stand in a single heap ... As soon as the bearers of the Ark reached the Jordan, and the feet of the priests bearing the Ark dipped into the water at its edge ... the waters ... piled up ... The priests who bore the Ark of the Lord's Covenant stood on dry land exactly in the middle of the Jordan, while all Israel crossed over on dry land, until the entire nation finished crossing the Jordan" (3, 13-17; see also 4, 18). The rod,

---

23   See above, pp. 9-10.
24   See S. E. Loewenstamm, *The Tradition of the Exodus in its Development*, Jerusalem 1965, pp. 103-105 (Hebrew).

dangerously analogous to a sort of magic wand, is replaced here by the Ark of the Lord, leaving no room for any misunderstanding: it is God Himself who performs the miracle.[25] Although here the priests assist God, the glory is all Joshua's: "On that day the Lord exalted Joshua in the sight of all Israel, so that they revered him all his days as they had revered Moses" (4, 14).

When God promises Joshua to deliver the city of Ai into his hands, He commands him: " . . . Hold out the javelin in your hand toward Ai . . . So Joshua held out the javelin in his hand toward the city. As soon as he held out his hand, the ambush came rushing out of their station. They entered the city and captured it . . . " (Jos. 8, 18-19). According to these verses, Joshua's act is nothing but a signal to those hiding in ambush to attack the city; the reader, however, cannot avoid the association with a similar story in which Moses plays the main role and Joshua a minor one—the war with Amalek (Ex. 17, 8-16). Despite the clear resemblance, a fundamental difference distinguishes the actions of the two leaders: Moses' act is a miraculous one and determines the course of the battle: "Then, whenever Moses held up his hand, Israel prevailed; but whenever he let down his hand, Amalek prevailed" (Ex. 17, 11). The object that assists Moses in performing the miracle is not a weapon, like the javelin, but the famous miraculous object, the rod of God (vs. 9). The miraculous trend nonetheless found its place in the continuation of Joshua's rationalistic story: "Joshua did not draw back the hand with which he held out his javelin until all the inhabitants of Ai had been exterminated" (vs. 26). This verse lends new meaning to Joshua's gesture, which must last until the battle ends: it becomes a miracle identical to that of Moses. What's more, this verse, which is not represented in the Septuagint,

---

25   It seems that the ark replaced the rod, which fell out of favor as it came to be seen as a magic object. For the magical nature of the rod, see Loewenstamm (n. 24), pp. 66-69.

interrupts the natural continuity between the number of casualties, reported in verse 25, and the booty taken by the Israelites in verse 27. Verse 26 is thus an interpolation which was added to the story in order to change the nature of Joshua's act and create greater resemblance between Joshua and his master.[26]

The biblical tendency to liken Joshua to Moses continued in the Second Temple period as well. The short scene in which the captain of the Lord tells Joshua, "Remove your sandal from your foot, for the place where you stand is holy" (Jos. 5, 13-15) is mainly built from materials typical to Second Temple biblical literature:[27]

a. "he looked up and saw" (in theophanies; vs. 13); compare Zec. 2, 1, 5; 5, 1, 5, 9; 6, 1; Dan. 8, 3; 10, 5; 1 Chr. 21, 16;

b. "and behold, a man" (after "and saw . . . "; vs. 13); compare, for instance, Zec. 2, 5;

c. "standing before him" (vs. 13); compare Dan. 8, 15;

d. "drawn sword in hand" (vs. 13); Nu. 22, 23, 31;[28] 1 Chr. 21, 16;

e. "I am the captain of the Lord's host" (vs. 14); see Dan. 8, 11;

f. "Now I have come" (vs. 14); see Dan. 9, 22-23;

g. "What does my lord command his servant?" (vs. 14); see Dan. 10, 17.

The writer of this short episode has Joshua experience a theophany before the conquest of the first city taken by the Israelites in Canaan, similar to the first theophany Moses

---

26 See Y. Amit, "And Joshua stretched out the Javelin that was at his Hand (Jos. 8, 19, 26)," *Shnaton, An Annual for Biblical and Ancient Near Eastern Studies* 5-6 (1978-1979), pp. 11-18 (Hebrew).

27 A. B. Ehrlich, *Mikra ki-Pheschuto*, vol. 2, Berlin 1900, p. 12 (Hebrew).

28 The story of Balaam's she-ass was also composed during the Second Temple period, see Rofé, (n. 7), especially pp. 54-57.

receives on the threshold of his mission.[29] There are a number of motives behind the addition of the theophany, which likens Joshua to Moses:

a. It explains the proscription (חרם) of Jericho (6, 17) in its holiness; see the word "holy" (קדש) in 6, 19; compare Lev. 27, 21, 28 (Abarbanel).

b. It explains that the Ark of God in chapter 6 functions as the "Ark of the Covenant of the Lord of Hosts" (compare, for instance 1 Sam. 4, 4).

c. It expresses the idea that the angel is involved in conquering the land (see Ex. 23, 20, 23; 33, 2).

d. The added scene is also related to the previous narrative, that of the circumcision of the Israelites. When Joshua sees the angel "drawn sword in hand" (וחרבו שלופה בידו), he asks him: "Are you one of us or our enemies?" (הלנו אתה אם לצרינו; vs. 13), words which remind us of God's command to Joshua: "Make flint swords (חרבות צרים) and proceed with a second circumcision of the Israelites" (vs. 2; see also vs. 3). The threatening picture of the angel, "drawn sword in hand," as it is associated with the circumcision in the previous chapter, reminds us of the foreboding theophany of Moses on his way back to Egypt to begin his mission, a drama which ends well only after a circumcision (Ex. 4, 24-26). We find a similarly dangerous meeting between a man/angel and a figure about to enter the land of Canaan in Genesis 32, 25-33. Kimhi, in his commentary on Joshua 5, 13, notes the parallel: " . . . as he was seen by Jacob our father and wrestled with him to strengthen him and to bring him the good news, as he told him: 'for you have striven . . . ' . . . And so this angel appeared to Joshua, drawn sword in hand . . . "

---

29   The nouns are in singular form—"sandal," "foot"—but in many manuscripts and in the Syriac version they are plural. In Exodus 3, 5 on the other hand, the nouns are in plural form—but in the Septuagint, the Vulgate and some manuscripts of the Samaritan Pentateuch they are singular.

Not all the resemblances created between Moses and Joshua add a positive dimension to the disciple's image. Such is the case when Joshua parallels Moses by sending spies to Canaan before he begins its conquest. The story of Joshua's spies to Jericho (Jos. 2) borrows from the story of Moses' spies, serving as its contrast in many ways.

The beginning of Joshua 2 already hints that something has gone wrong: the initiative to send the spies is not God's (see Nu. 13, 1) but Joshua's, a sign of its unnecessariness. The sense of impending failure is magnified by the anonymous characterization of the spies as "two men." Aristocratic origin does not necessarily promise success, but biblical espionage stories make clear that spies worth their name must come from good families: "each one a chieftain among them" (Nu. 13, 2), "all the men being leaders of the Israelites" (vs. 3; see also Jud. 18, 2; 2 Sam. 15, 35-36). The spies Joshua selects are neither nobles nor men of valor; he apparently nabbed the first two lads who happened to be near his tent when he initially thought to send spies to Jericho.

Joshua's negligence does not end with the selection; it continues with the way he instructs them in preparation for the mission. In contrast to Moses, who presents a long list of strategic and geo-political issues which were to be examined by the spies (Nu. 13, 17-20; see also Dt. 1, 22), Joshua, whose words initially resemble those of Moses, sends the spies without any guidance: "Go to the land and Jericho" (vs. 1). Such an opening to the story—inexperienced spies of undistinguished backgrounds sent on their mission with no instruction—promises the reader an extraordinary story and even a humorous one; hence, we are hardly surprised when, instead of doing their job, the two immediately enter the house of a prostitute and news of their presence and intentions becomes common knowledge the moment they reach the city gates.

When Rahab hides the spies from the king's messengers, the word used by the author is "hidden" (ותצפנו; vs. 4), reminding us of the story of baby Moses being hidden by his mother: "she

65

hid him for three months" (ותצפנהו שלושה ירחים; Ex. 2, 2); the verb צפ"ן occurs in biblical prose only in these two stories! This detail also arouses laughter—the spies depend on this woman who treats them like babies.

Joshua sent spies in spite of God's promise to give the land to the Israelites (1, 2-4); it is the prostitute, however, who expresses certainty of God's promise and mentions His past victory over the Egyptians during the Exodus: "For we have heard how the Lord dried up the waters of the Sea of Reeds for you when you left Egypt" (vs. 10). Moreover, the irony becomes overt when Rahab actually quotes from the Song of the Sea in order to point out how frightened the Canaanites are: "All the dwellers of Canaan are aghast/Terror and dread descend upon them" (Ex. 15, 15-16); "Because dread of you has descended upon us/And all the dwellers of the land are aghast before you" (Jos. 2, 9). Note the chiastic order, typical of inner-biblical quotations.[30]

We would expect Joshua to know more than a prostitute from Jericho; must he learn his lesson in trusting God's promises from such a woman? Yet that is just what happens. His two spies return and repeat the words of Rahab: " . . . The Lord has delivered the whole land into our power; in fact all the inhabitants of the land are aghast before us" (vs. 24). Joshua, whose act was completely unnecessary and negligent, received a perfect report in the end, better than that brought by Moses' highly respectable spies (among them Joshua) who, though properly guided, misrepresented the land they had scouted and frightened the Israelites (Nu. 13, 26-33).

The story of Joshua's spies is a parody of espionage stories, especially the story of Moses' spies. God's intention to help

[30]　See M. Seidel, "Parallels between the Book of Isaiah and the Book of Psalms," *Hiqre Mikra*, Jerusalem 1978, pp. 1-97 (Hebrew); R. Weiss, "Chiasmus in the Bible," *Studies in the Text and Language of the Bible*, Jerusalem 1981, pp. 155-158 (Hebrew).

the Israelites remains unaltered despite Joshua's deviation from the correct behavior of Moses, and the land is eventually delivered into their hands. Joshua, who should have trusted God's promise, in the end learns his lesson through unrespectable agents; the prostitute and her family, whose lives were spared by Joshua, serve as an eternal reminder of that lesson.[31]

Gideon's awareness of the tension between God's past acts of salvation during the Exodus (Jud. 6, 13) and those of his own time has already been mentioned.[32] Gideon's personality and life story are in many ways a reflection of the Moses traditions:

a. Gideon's request for signs (Jud. 6, 36-40) reminds us of the signs given to Moses preceding his acceptance of his mission (Ex. 4, 1-9).

b. Gideon's attempt to evade the mission, "Please, my lord, how can I deliver Israel? Why, my clan is the humblest in Manasseh, and I am the youngest in my father's household" (6, 15), has much in common with Moses' words: "Who am I that I should go to Pharaoh and free the Israelites from Egypt?" (Ex. 3, 11). God's answer to Moses there: "I will be with you . . . " (vs. 12) is paralleled verbatim in His answer to Gideon: "I will be with you . . . " (6, 16).

c. Gideon expresses his fear when he realizes he saw an angel: "Alas, O Lord God! for I have seen an angel of the Lord face to face" (6, 22). Moses exhibits a similar reaction to the theophany he experiences: "And Moses hid his face, for he was afraid to look at God" (Ex. 3, 6).

---

31 For a close reading of this narrative, see Y. Zakovitch, "Humor and Theology, or the Successful Failure of the Israelite Intelligence: A Literary Folkloric Approach to Jos. 2," in *Text and Tradition. The Hebrew Bible and Folklore (SBL Semeia Studies)*, ed. by S. Niditch, Atlanta 1990, pp. 75-98.

32 See pp. 48-49.

d. The verb "to rebuke" (ריב), which expresses the complaint of the men of Ephraim against Gideon ("And they rebuked him severely" [Jud. 8, 1]), serves as a covert name derivation of the figure's other name, Jerubbaal (ירבעל).[33] It refers, as well, to the people's complaints against Moses in the wilderness: "The people rebuked [with] Moses . . . and Moses replied to them, 'Why do you rebuke [with] me . . . ' " (Ex. 17, 2; see also vs. 7).

e. A significant resemblance can be traced between the story of the ephod made by Gideon (Jud. 8, 24-27) and the story of the Golden Calf (Ex. 32). In its present form, the story condemns Gideon for building the ephod. The verb used to characterize the people's consent has strong negative connotations, usually associated with idolatry, "There all Israel went astray (ויזנו) after it" (vs. 27a[b]), and their sin is followed by the punishment of Gideon and his family: "And it became a snare to Gideon and his house" (vs. 27b). In its original form, the story seems to have been more in Gideon's favor: it is improbable that after declaring his refusal to rule over Israel ("I will not rule over you myself . . . the Lord alone shall rule over you" [vs. 23]) he would dare turn around and tempt the children of Israel to worship idols. Thus, in the original version of the story, the ephod was apparently a legitimate instrument used to seek information from God (see 1 Sam. 14, 3 [also in vs. 18 according to some Septuagint manuscripts]; 23, 6-9; 30, 7).[34] The fact that the story reminds the reader of the Golden Calf tradition, through the golden earrings from which both the ephod and the calf are built (Ex. 32, 2-3; Jud. 8, 24-26), and through the reference to the sins of the Israelites later in the chapter (including the verb "went astray"—ויזנו; vss. 33-35), caused the interpolation of verse 27a[b]-b, which in

33 For another derivation of the name Jerubbaal from ריב, see Judges 6, 31-32.
34 On the ephod as a legitimate oracular instrument, see C. F. Burney, *The Book of Judges*, Oxford 1918, p. 243.

turn changed the meaning of the scene. The addition of these words serves to combine the Gideon story with the subsequent chapter, chapter 9, the story of Abimelech, thereby justifying the tragic fate of Gideon's house. Disconnected from its context, one would not suspect that the Abimelech story was written in order to supply a punishment for Gideon. Here, Gideon has the reputation of a righteous person, as we see especially in verses 16-17: "Now then, if you acted honorably and loyally in making Abimelech king, if you have done right by Jerubbaal and his house and have requited him according to his deserts—considering that my father fought for you and saved you from the Midianites at the risk of his life." Moreover, the end of chapter 8 does not even hint that making the ephod was a sin: "The Israelites gave no thought to the Lord their God, who saved them from all the enemies around them. Nor did they show loyalty to the house of Jerubbaal-Gideon in return for all the good that he had done for Israel" (vss. 34-35).

The redactor who added words to the ephod story concerned himself with the principle of divine retribution, wishing to justify God for the calamity brought upon Gideon's house. He was thus compelled to show that Gideon, the savior of Israel, deserved to be punished. This caused him to alter the ephod story, making it a refection of the Golden Calf story and turning Gideon into an anti-Mosaic character.

The prophet Elijah is indeed a second Moses. The books of the later prophets as a whole are sealed with the invocation of both figures: "Be mindful of the teaching of My servant Moses, whom I charged at Horeb with laws and rules for all Israel. Lo, I will send the prophet Elijah to you before the coming of the awesome, fearful day of the Lord. He shall reconcile parents with children and children with their parents, so that when I come, I do not strike the whole land with utter destruction" (Mal. 3, 22-24). When prophecy is no longer part of their reality, the Israelites' only remaining source of guidance is the holy book—the Law of Moses. Elijah alone, of all the

69

prophets, can reappear before them, since he did not die but ascended to heaven. It is he, ultimately, who will return the Israelites to Mosaic law.

Consequent to the declaration of Elijah, "As the Lord lives, the God of Israel whom I serve, there will be no dew or rain except at my bidding" (1 Ki. 17, 1), God sustains the prophet during the drought: "The ravens brought him bread and meat every morning and every evening, and he drank from the wadi" (vs. 6). This miracle reminds the reader of the manna and quail miracles in the wilderness, suggested in Moses' words: " . . . who will give you flesh to eat in the evening and bread in the morning to the full . . . " (Ex. 16, 8). In the Septuagint to Kings, the similarity to Exodus is even more marked: "The ravens brought him bread every morning and meat in the evening." The manna and quail miracles were performed to test the Israelites and train them in observing the commandments,[35] but they failed the test. The reader of Kings is reminded of the Moses stories and realizes that the moral state of the Israelites has deteriorated still further: they have fallen to Baal worship, and only the prophet himself is worthy of help during the drought.

The story of Elijah in Horeb (1 Ki. 19) is built from motifs borrowed from the Moses cycle. What is Elijah doing at Horeb? The mountain has an illustrious history—there Moses sees God as he tends Jethro's flock, and he climbs to its summit to receive the divine Law. Elijah's arena, on the other hand, is the land of Israel; if he suddenly makes his way to Mount Horeb, we must seek the meaning of this surprising journey. The suggestion is subtle: the reader is aroused to question the kinship between Moses and Elijah.

Elijah is graced with a metabolic miracle—he walks without eating or drinking for forty days until he reaches Mount Horeb (vs. 8), a clear reflection of Moses' ascent of Mount Horeb and the period of forty days and forty nights he

35   See pp. 110-111.

remains there when he receives the Law (Ex. 24, 18). Yet the Elijah story has even more to do with Moses' second encounter with God, at his reception of the second tablets: "and he was there with the Lord forty days and forty nights; he ate no bread and drank no water; and he wrote down on the tablets the terms of the covenant . . . " (Ex. 34, 28; see also Dt. 9, 9, 18).

God's revelation to Elijah also follows the lines of the revelation to Moses.[36] Moses stands in "a cleft of the rock" (Ex. 33, 22) and Elijah, likewise, stands "at the entrance of the cave" (1 Ki. 19, 13). The author mentions a specific cave rather than simply "a cave" because he identifies Elijah's cave with Moses' cleft of the rock, an identification known in rabbinic literature (BT *Pesahim* 54a; see also *Megillah* 19b). At the outset of the theophany, Elijah is commanded to leave the cave and watch God's passing by (vs. 11), which reminds the reader of Exodus 33, 19: "I will make all My goodness pass before you . . . "[37] God covers Moses' eyes to hide His countenance from him: "and, as My Presence passes by, I will put you in a cleft of the rock and shield you with My hand until I have passed by. Then I will take My hand away and you will see My back; but My face must not be seen" (vss. 22-23); Elijah covers his own eyes: "When Elijah heard it [God's voice], he wrapped his mantle about his face" (vs. 13).

The entire literary complex of Exodus 32-34 describes the terrible split between God and His people, the worshipers of the Golden Calf. It is a crisis that continues until the renewal of the covenant, and its spirit seems to sweep over 1 Kings 19 as well.[38] The resemblance between the narratives is purposeful: it prompts a comparison between the behavior of the two

---

36 See G. Fohrer, *Elia*, ATHANT 31, Zürich 1957, pp. 48-49.
37 An assimilation of the preparations for the theophany took place in the Septuagint: the word "tomorrow" was added to 1 Kings 19, 11, and see Exodus 34, 2.
38 On the unity imposed by the redactor on Exodus 32-34 see B. S. Childs, *Exodus (OTL)*, London 1975, p. 597.

leaders, Moses and Elijah, during a crisis of faith. The comparison does not flatter Elijah. When the sin of the people is discovered, God threatens to destroy them and make of Moses a great nation (Ex. 32, 10), but Moses pleads in the name of Israel and does not cease until God grants his request: "and the Lord renounced the punishment He had planned to bring upon His people" (32, 14; compare Dt. 9, 25-29). Moses then wants to atone for the people's sins and does not hesitate to endanger his own life: "Now, if You will forgive their sin [well and good]; but if not, erase me from the record which You have written" (vs. 32). Elijah asks God to take his life because he despairs of his people and his prophetic mission (1 Ki. 19, 4). Moses, on the other hand, considers his life devoid of meaning if God will not forgive his people.

The revelation in Exodus 33 is initiated by Moses, who asks for a sign that the people have regained God's favor (vs. 16). God grants his request, thereby manifesting His attribute of mercy: "and He answered, 'I will make all My goodness pass before you, and I will proclaim before you the name Lord, and the grace that I grant and the compassion that I show'" (vs. 19). When God passes by Moses, Israel's advocate, we read: "The Lord came down in a cloud; He stood with him there, and proclaimed the name Lord. The Lord passed before him and proclaimed: The Lord! The Lord! A God compassionate and gracious, slow to anger, abounding in kindness and faithfulness, extending kindness to the thousandth generation, forgiving iniquity, transgression, and sin . . ." (34, 5-7). But an opposing divine attribute, that of strict justice, is given expression as well: " . . . yet He does not remit all punishment, but visits the iniquity of parents upon children and children's children, upon the third and fourth generations" (ibid.). Moses, who considers himself one of the people, hastens to ask: "If I have gained Your favor, O Lord, pray let the Lord go in our midst, even though this is a stiff-necked people. Pardon our iniquity and our sin, and take us for Your own" (vs. 9). God grants Moses' request and tells him: "I hereby make a covenant. Before all your people I will work such wonders . . . " (vs. 10). This covenant places some responsibilities upon the people: loyalty to God and war against idolatry: " . . . You must tear down their altars, smash their pillars, and cut down their sacred posts; for you must not worship any other god, because the Lord, whose name is impassioned, is an impassioned God" (34, 13-14; compare Ex. 20, 5). In the Elijah narrative, the Israelites have indeed forsaken the covenant (1 Ki. 19, 10). Rather than destroying the altars to foreign gods, they have destroyed God's own altar (ibid.) and have even bowed down to Baal (vs. 18) despite the strict prohibition. The people's conduct arouses Elijah's wrath: "I am moved by zeal to the Lord . . . " (vs. 10). The covenant made in forgiveness of the sin of the Golden Calf has been broken, but Elijah's reaction stands in stark contrast to that of Moses. The later prophet announces Israel's sins, declares God's zeal, and calls for revenge! Against the background of Exodus 32-34 the contrast between Moses, the model prophet, and Elijah is pronounced: Elijah, Israel's prosecutor, deviated from his mission as a prophet and advocate of Israel.[39]

The tradition of Elijah's ascent to heaven also borrows from the Mosaic narratives: not from the written version of Moses' death found in Deuteronomy 34, but from an earlier stratum of the tradition. The book of Kings does not hesitate to relate that Elijah was still alive when he was taken to heaven, but we must realize that the text does not preserve the Elijah ascent tradition in its full glory. Only one verse speaks of the ascent itself: "As they kept on walking and talking, a fiery chariot with fiery horses suddenly appeared and separated one from the other, and Elijah went up to heaven in a whirlwind" (2 Ki. 2, 11). This dearth of information is due to the fact that 2 Kings 2 is dedicated to the figure of Elisha; the message of this chapter's story is that "the spirit of Elijah

39   On the message of 1 Kings 19 see Y. Zakovitch, "A Still Small Voice," *Tarbiz* 51 (1982), pp. 329-346 (Hebrew).

has settled on Elisha" (vs. 15).[40] Elijah's miracle of immortality reaches us only through the back door—evidence of the unease writers felt about the immortality of some holy men.

Loewenstamm has already suggested the possibility that a similar story of ascension was told about Moses, and that the authorized tradition in Deuteronomy 34, "no one knows his burial place to this day" (vs. 6), echoes that older tradition and polemicizes against it.[41] The contention that Moses did not die is voiced by Josephus Flavius: " ... a cloud stood over him on the sudden, and he disappeared in a certain valley, although he wrote in the holy books that he died, which was done out of fear, lest they should venture to say that, because of his extraordinary virtue, he went to God" (*Ant.*, 4, 8, 48). A similar supposition appears in the Talmud where Moses stands and serves God in heaven (BT *Sotah* 13b).

Interestingly, the place from which Elijah ascends to heaven—the far side of the Jordan, opposite Jericho—is the same place mentioned in the story of Moses' death: "Moses went up from the steppes of Moab to Mount Nebo, to the summit of Pisgah, opposite Jericho, and the Lord showed him the whole land ... " (Dt. 34, 1). This phenomenon of traditions and their transformations may be illustrated in the realm of astronomy: the light of a distant star may reach us long after the star itself has ceased to exist, due to the time light takes to travel between its source and our planet. In the same way, the original story of Moses' ascent has disappeared, but its light still shines in the Elijah story.

The relationship between Elisha and Elijah mirrors that between Joshua and Moses. In both, the disciple follows his mentor. The nature of this link between Elisha and Elijah is

40 A. Rofé, *The Prophetical Stories*, Jerusalem 1988, pp. 44-45.
41 S. E. Loewenstamm, "The Death of Moses," in *Studies on the Testament of Abraham*, ed. G. W. E. Nickelsburg Jr, Montana 1976, pp. 185-217.

attested in two traditions: that of their first meeting (1 Ki. 19, 19-21) and the above-mentioned story in which the spirit of Elijah settles on Elisha (2 Ki. 2, 1-18). It is no coincidence that a double miracle of crossing the Jordan marks the changing of the guards in this story: Elijah crosses the Jordan on dry land, returning to the site of Moses' death, and Elisha repeats his master's miracle, crossing the Jordan to Canaan, like Joshua, where he begins to fulfill his mission.

The story of Elisha curing the water of Jericho (2 Ki. 2, 19-22) strongly resembles the story of Moses curing the waters of Marah (Ex. 15, 22-26), although the message of the two narratives differs greatly. The Marah story carries a clear theological message:[42] in Exodus 15 "the people grumbled against Moses, saying 'What shall we drink?' " (vs. 24), but Moses expresses his helplessness by crying out to God (vs. 25) who directs him to the solution: "And the Lord showed him a piece of wood; he threw it into the water and the water became sweet" (ibid.). In the Jericho story, on the other hand, the prophet, and the people's admiration for him,[43] become the focus. The men of the town respect Elisha and politely tell him: "Look, the town is a pleasant place to live in, as my lord can see; but the water is bad and the land causes bereavement" (2 Ki. 2, 19). Elisha himself solves the problem without a moment's hesitation: "He responded, 'Bring me a new dish and put salt in it.' They brought it to him; he went to the spring and threw salt into it" (vs. 20-21a). Only then does Elisha mention God and relate the miracle to Him: "and he said, 'Thus said the Lord: I heal this water; no longer shall death and bereavement come from it!' " (vs. 21b). When the writer tells us that the declaration was carried into effect, however, he mentions not God but the prophet: "The water has

42 See pp. 109-110.
43 So also in other stories of the Elisha cycle; see 4, 1-7; 4, 38-41; 6, 1-7.

remained wholesome to this day, in accordance with the word spoken by Elisha" (vs. 22).[44]

In the war of the three kings against Moab (2 Ki. 3), unbearable thirst endangers the army: " . . . and there was no water left for the army or for the animals that were with them" (vs. 9). We must compare this with the accounts of the Israelite wanderings in the wilderness (Ex. 17, 3; Nu. 20, 4). Elisha's solution involves an optical illusion: the sun, rising over the water, will paint it red. This mirage misleads the Moabites: "Next morning, when they rose, the sun was shining over the water, and from the distance the water appeared to the Moabites as red as blood. 'That is blood!' they said. 'The kings must have fought among themselves and killed each other. Now to the spoil, Moab!' " (vss. 22-23).

This element in the story reminds the reader of the two stories in which Moses transmutes water to blood. The first is the story of the blood sign: " . . . take some water from the Nile and pour it on the dry ground, and the water you take from the Nile will turn to blood on dry ground" (Ex. 4, 9). The second is the account of the first plague: "Thus said the Lord, 'By this you shall know that I am the Lord.' See, I shall strike the water in the Nile with the rod that is in my hand, and it will be turned into blood . . . " (Ex. 7, 17; read through vs. 24). The link between these stories was picked up by Josephus Flavius, who tends generally to give miracle stories rationalistic interpretations. Here, he tells these two Exodus blood stories in the spirit of 2 Kings 3 (*Ant.*, 2, 12, 3; 2, 14, 1).[45]

44 For a comparison of these two stories in the midrash, see *Tanhuma, Beshallah* 24a.

45 An additional example of rationalization of a miraculous motif can be traced in another Elisha story: his promise of food for the besieged people of Samaria. Elisha says: "Hear the word of the Lord. Thus said the Lord: This time tomorrow, a seah of choice flour shall sell for a shekel at the gate of Samaria, and two seahs of barley for a shekel" (2 Ki. 7, 1). The king's aide mocks the prophet and understands his words as if they referred to a

Elisha heals the leprosy of Naaman, the commander of the army of the king of Aram, and the disease clings to Gehazi, Elisha's attendant (2 Ki. 5). Naaman recognizes the prophet's authority and the power of God following the miracle (see especially his declaration in vs. 14), but Gehazi, who rebels against the authority of his master and pursues Naaman's wealth, is punished: "Surely the leprosy of Naaman shall cling to you and to your descendants forever" (vs. 27).

Two other biblical leprosy narratives dealing with the cause and cure of the disease are associated with Moses (Ex. 4, 6-7; Nu. 12, 1-16). The first story tells of the leprosy sign given to Moses in response to his anxiety that the people will not recognize his authority as God's messenger (vs. 1). The double sign—the appearance and disappearance of the disease—ensures the people's belief in the prophet (vs. 8). This story, like that of Naaman, thus concerns questions of recognizing authority, but here the leprosy is merely a sign and not a punishment: God gives the sign and the prophet is passive, symbolizing with his body the authority of his Lord. While in 2 Kings 5 the person smitten with leprosy is not the one who is cured, in Exodus 4 Moses is the subject of both stages. Exodus 4, 6-7 and 2 Kings 5 share some expressions: "his hand was encrusted with snowy scales" (Ex. 4, 6), "and as [Gehazi] left his presence, he was encrusted with snowy scales" (2 Ki. 5, 27); ". . . there it was restored like his flesh" (Ex. 4, 7); ". . . and your flesh shall be restored" (2 Ki. 5, 10; see also vs. 14).

The story of Numbers 12 is likewise about prophetic authority. Miriam and Aaron doubt their subordination to Moses:

> miracle like the manna, "bread from heaven" given in the wilderness (Ex. 16, 4; Ps. 105, 40; Neh. 9, 15): "Even if the Lord were to make windows in the sky, could this come to pass?" (vs. 2). But Samaria is promised food in plenty because of the hasty retreat of the Aramean army; they flee in terror because "the Lord had caused the Aramean camp to hear a sound of chariots, a sound of horses . . . And they fled headlong in the twilight, abandoning their tents and horses and asses . . . " (vss. 6-7).

77

"They said, 'Has the Lord spoken only through Moses? Has He not spoken through us as well?' " (vs. 2). Miriam receives the same punishment as Gehazi, but she is cured by grace of Moses' intervention and prayer for her. The authority she questioned was that of Moses rather than God's, but she is punished in order to bring her to realize her subordination to the prophet, her brother. Moses intercedes for her, demonstrating to Miriam that only he (and not she or Aaron) can serve as mediator, by bringing God to cure her.[46]

The story of Elisha's burial and the resurrection miracle that takes place on his grave (2 Ki. 13, 20-21) is highly exceptional: a prophet dies, no grief is aroused, and an unimpressive burial follows, along with a miracle that is seen by no witnesses and in which God seems to play no role. The miracle is not even necessary; the person brought back to life gives no sign of his gratitude, and the site where the miracle was performed is unknown, never becoming an attraction for pilgrims. In brief, this miracle leaves no impression, and the narrator makes no attempt to establish its credibility.

It is interesting that such a ludicrous story, which belittles the image of the prophet, nonetheless shares some elements with the story of Moses' death in Deuteronomy 34 that we have already compared with the story of Elijah's ascent. The place of Moses' burial is unknown (Dt. 34, 6) for the same reason that no direct information is given about the location of Elisha's burial: to prevent a cult of graves. However, the comparison to the Moses story explains why "bands of Moabites" pass by Elisha's grave: Moses and Elisha left this world in the very same place!

Another similarity between the two stories is their avoidance of naming the agents who buried the two prophets: "He buried him in the valley" (Dt. 34, 6); "and they buried him" (2 Ki. 13, 20). But while in Deuteronomy one may assume that it

---

46   In 2 Chronicles 26, 16-21 Uzziah is punished with leprosy because he does not respect priestly authority.

was God who buried Moses (see vs. 5: "So Moses . . . died there . . . at the command of the Lord"), the anonymity of those burying Elisha suits the story's minimalism—the whole episode is not important enough to treat at length. That is why no one really mourns the death of Elisha, while "the Israelites bewailed Moses in the steppes of Moab for thirty days" (vs. 8). A further element in Deuteronomy 34 that glorifies Moses to the detriment of Elisha is Moses' death in good health at the age of one hundred and twenty years (vs. 7). Elisha dies like any ordinary person because "he had been stricken with the illness of which he was to die" (vs. 14). The story of Elisha's death thus stands in the shadow of Moses' death story (and the story of Elijah's ascent).

We have already considered the assumption that the original tradition about Moses' disappearance from our world ended not with his death and burial but with his ascent to heaven. In the Elisha story there is an immortality element as well; it is not the prophet who is resurrected, however, but an anonymous person whose life is of no importance in the narrative.[47] Though the story of Moses' death may be a polemic with the tradition that he became immortal, the writer nonetheless expresses great admiration for Moses. The story in the book of Kings, on the other hand, treats Elisha quite cruelly.

Let us return now from the realm of prophecy to the realm of kingship: Moses and David are both shepherds taken from their woolly flocks to lead their people. Moses shows his leadership potential when he rescues the daughters of Jethro

---

[47] For various options in interpreting this short story, see Y. Zakovitch, " 'Elisha Died . . . He Came to Life and Stood Up' (2 Ki. 13, 20-21): A Short, Short Story in Exegetical Circles" in "Sha'arei Talmon": Studies in the Bible, Qumran, and the Ancient Near East Presented to Shemaryahu Talmon, ed. by M. Fishbane and E. Tov with the assistance of W. Fields, Winona Lake, Indiana 1991, pp. 53-62.

from the other shepherds and waters their flock (Ex. 2, 16-19). As he watches over Jethro's grazing flock, God reveals Himself to Moses and appoints him for the mission of saving the Israelites (3, 1).

The midrash makes the overt connection between Moses the shepherd and Moses the leader:

> Also Moses was tested by God through sheep. Our Rabbis said that when Moses our teacher, peace be upon him, was tending the flock of Jethro in the wilderness, a little kid escaped from him. He ran after it until it reached a shady place. When it reached the shady place, there appeared to view a pool of water and the kid stopped to drink. When Moses approached it, he said: "I did not know that you ran away because of thirst; you must be weary." So he placed the kid on his shoulder and walked away. Thereupon God said: "Because thou hast mercy in leading the flock of a mortal, thou will assuredly tend my flock Israel." Hence "Now Moses was keeping the flock." [*Exodus Rabbah*, ed. by H. Freedman and M. Simon, (London 1939), 2, 2 (p. 49)]

As for David, the link between pasturing his flock and caring for his people as a shepherd is made in the Bible itself: "I took you from the pasture, from following the flock, to be ruler of My people Israel" (2 Sam. 7, 8; see also 5, 2). The point is made especially in Psalm 78, 70-72: "He chose David, His servant, and took him from the sheepfolds. He brought him from minding the nursing ewes to tend His people Jacob, Israel, His very own. He tended them with blameless heart, with skillful hands he led them."

It is worthy of note that this historical psalm deals extensively with God's supreme act of grace—the Exodus—and with the ingratitude of the Israelites (= the Ephraimites; vs. 9): the Israelites do not keep the covenant of God despite the many miracles performed for them (vss. 9-39) and despite God's destruction of their enemies (vss. 40-55). As a result, Israel is represented as an enemy of God (see vs. 66). The psalm mentions no Israelite leader—not even Moses. God Himself is the shepherd of the Israelites: "He set His people moving like sheep, drove them like a flock in the wilderness. He led them in safety; they were unafraid . . . " (vss. 52-53). The verb "led" is related to God once again in verse 14 and to David in verse 72. The verb "drove" appears in relation to Moses pasturing his flock in Exodus 3, 1: "Now Moses, tending the flock of his father-in-law Jethro, the priest of Midian, drove the flock into the wilderness . . . " According to Psalm 78, Israel (the northern kingdom) loses God's favor because of its continual ingratitude from the outset of the Exodus. God chooses Judah and Jerusalem (vss. 67-69), and David is the one and only human leader who inherits God's role of leading the people of Israel.

David himself makes the analogy between his ability to protect his flock from the beasts and to save Israel by killing Goliath: " . . . Your servant has been tending his father's sheep, and if a lion or a bear came and carried off an animal from the flock, I would go after it and fight and rescue it from its mouth . . . Your servant has killed both lion and bear; and that uncircumcised Philistine shall end up like one of them . . . " (1 Sam. 17, 34-37).

The apocryphal psalm from Qumran (Ps. 151) also makes the connection between David as shepherd of his flock and shepherd of his people:

Smaller was I than my brothers
and the youngest of the sons of my father,
So he made me shepherd of his flock
and ruler over his kids . . .
But he sent and took me from behind the flock
and anointed me with holy oil,
and he made me leader of his people
and ruler over the sons of his covenant.
[J. A. Sanders, *The Psalms Scroll of Qumran, Cave 11*,
(Oxford 1965), pp. 55-56; note the repetition of the word "ruler"!)]

81

The midrash emphasizes the similarity between the two shepherds, Moses and David: "Here you have two great leaders whom God first proved by a little thing, found trustworthy, and then promoted to greatness. He tested David with sheep which he led through the wilderness ... Similarly in the case of Moses ... " (*Exodus Rabbah* [op. cit., p. 80], p. 49).

The book of Ruth, a late composition that did not find its way to its natural location following the book of Judges,[48] completes what is lacking in the book of Samuel by supplying a very respectable genealogy for David. The genealogy spans ten generations (4, 18-22) and stands at the end of the book of Ruth, which is an Exodus-like story.

a. The book begins with the family's abandoning the country because of hunger: " ... there was a famine in the land ... ,"a clear association with the story of Abraham's descent to Egypt (Gen. 12, 10; see also 26, 1). A similar phrase appears in the story leading to the descent of Jacob's family to Egypt (see Gen. 41, 54; 43, 1; Ps. 105, 16).

b. The phrase "went to sojourn" (vs. 1) also carries us back to the Exodus pattern: see "to sojourn there" (Gen. 12, 10); "We have come ... to sojourn in the land" (Gen. 47, 4; see also Isa. 52, 4).

c. During the family's sojourn in Moab, all its male members die (Ruth 1, 3, 5). In the Exodus story, Pharaoh commands every boy to be killed (Ex. 1, 16, 22).

d. Before they die, Elimelech's sons marry Moabite women (1, 4) like Joseph who marries an Egyptian woman (Gen. 41, 45). Moses, who escapes from Egypt to Midian, also marries the daughter of a local priest there (Ex. 2, 21).[49] That both Joseph and Moses had wives of noble standing led the midrash

---

48   See Y. Zakovitch, *Ruth—A Commentary. Mikra Leyisra'el,* Tel-Aviv–Jerusalem 1990, pp. 15-16 (Hebrew).

49   For more expressions of this element of the pattern, see, for example, pp. 92-94 and p. 118.

c. During the family's sojourn in Moab, all its male members die (Ruth 1, 3, 5). In the Exodus story, Pharaoh commands every boy to be killed (Ex. 1, 16, 22).

d. Before they die, Elimelech's sons marry Moabite women (1, 4) like Joseph who marries an Egyptian woman (Gen. 41, 45). Moses, who escapes from Egypt to Midian, also marries the daughter of a local priest there (Ex. 2, 21).[49] That both Joseph and Moses had wives of noble standing led the midrash to turn Naomi's daughters-in-law into Moabite princesses, the daughters of Eglon King of Moab (*Ruth Rabbah*, 2, 9).

e. After a long stay in the foreign country, the family (Naomi and her daughters-in-law) return to the land of Israel.

A resemblance to the Exodus narrative can also be found in the history of the young David when he is brought to Saul's court:

a. At the outset, David is warmly welcomed into the court of the king, as was Joseph into the court of Pharaoh, as well as heroes of other stories that follow the Exodus pattern: Jacob in Haran (see above) and Jeroboam and Adad in Egypt (see below).

b. David marries his host's daughter (1 Sam. 18, 17-28), as do Jacob, Adad and Jeroboam.

c. The host comes to hate his protégé and plots his death: Saul seeks to kill David (see for instance 1 Sam. 19, 2) like Pharaoh who wishes to kill Moses (Ex. 2, 15) and Solomon who seeks to execute Jeroboam (1 Ki. 11, 40).

d. The guest escapes from his host: David from Saul (1 Sam. 19, 12; 20, 1; 21, 11; 22, 17; 27, 1) like Moses (Ex. 2, 15) and Jeroboam (1 Ki. 11, 40) who flee from hostile kings.

e. When David escapes from Saul's court, Jonathan explains his absence to the king: "David begged leave of me to go to Bethlehem. He said, 'Please let me go (שלחני) for we are going

---

49 For more expressions of this element of the pattern, see, for example, pp. 92-94 and p. 118.

h. Pharaoh's capriciousness and inconsistency is paralleled in Saul's behavior (see for instance 1 Sam. 24, 17-22; 26, 17-25).

i. As Moses stays in Midian until the death of Pharaoh, so David remains in the Philistine kingdom until Saul's death (see 1 Sam. 30; 2 Sam. 1).

j. The entire biblical law is given to the Israelites by Moses. One law is given by David while he wanders with his people in flight from Saul (1 Sam. 30, 25), but it seems that this secondary verse (in any case similar to a law given by Moses in the wilderness [Nu. 31, 25-30]) was added to the story in order to present David as a legislator, a second Moses.[50]

The Amalekite issue plays an important role in the Exodus story (Ex. 17, 8-16; Nu. 14, 41-45; Dt. 25, 17-19)[51] and arouses expectations of revenge in the future—as, for example, in Exodus 17, 14-16, and especially in Deuteronomy 25, 19: "Therefore, when the Lord your God grants you safety from all your enemies around you . . . you shall blot out the memory of Amalek from under heaven. Do not forget!" The opportunity to fulfill this injunction is given to King Saul: "Thus said the Lord of Hosts: I am exacting the penalty for what Amalek did to Israel, for the assault he made upon them on the road, on their way to Egypt. Now go, attack Amalek, and proscribe all that belongs to him. Spare no one . . . " (1 Sam. 15, 2-3). Saul does not obey God and loses his kingdom to David: " . . . for you have rejected the Lord's command, and the Lord has rejected you as king over Israel . . . and Samuel said to him, 'The Lord has this day torn the kingship over Israel away from you and has given it to another who is worthier than you' " (vss. 26-28).

David is indeed the one who fulfills God's expectations for revenge: The story of Saul's death on Mount Gilboa (1 Sam. 31) stands between the story of the Amalekite raid of Ziklag, David's city (ch. 30), and the story about the young Amalekite

50   See pp. 112-113.
51   On the Amalek traditions, see more on pp. 119-121.

who comes to Ziklag to meet David after his return from defeating the Amalekites there, in order to bring the news that he has killed the king (2 Sam. 1).

The placement of Saul's death story between the two stories about David and the Amalekites is not accidental: Saul is in disgrace because of his Amalekite failure and Samuel reminds him of his sin before his last battle: "The Lord has torn the kingship out of your hands and has given it to your fellow, to David, because you did not obey the Lord and did not execute His wrath upon the Amalekites. That is why the Lord has done this to you today" (1 Sam. 28, 17-18).

The Amalekite framework around the story of Saul's death adds an important dimension to the comparison between Saul and David: in contrast to Saul, David is quick to castigate the Amalekites although he was not commanded to do so (ch. 30). He does not hesitate to kill the young Amalekite who brings him the news about Saul. The Amalekite's report adds an ironic dimension to the story: according to him, he himself—an Amalekite and an enemy—killed Saul, who had earlier spared the Amalekite's life! Moreover, the Amalekite revealed his identity to Saul, "and I told him I was an Amalekite" (2 Sam. 1, 8), and the king asks the Amalekite to kill him. Thus, according to this version, Saul brings upon himself the 'measure for measure' punishment he deserves. David, on the other hand, settles the account opened with the Exodus.[52]

In Second Temple biblical historiography, David's image changes: his role in religion and cult is emphasized through the preparations he made for the construction of the temple in Jerusalem and the organization of worship that would take place there.[53] David thus follows in the path of Moses, who

---

52 For the completion of the mission in the book of Esther, see pp. 54-55.

53 See S. Japhet, *The Ideology of the Book of Chronicles and its Place in Biblical Thought [Beiträge zur Erforschung des Alten*

played the main role in building the tabernacle. Consequently, David is called "a man of God" (Neh. 12, 24, 36; 2 Chr. 8, 14), an appellation shared by Moses (Dt. 33, 1; Ps. 90, 1; Ezr. 3, 2; 1 Chr. 23, 14; 2 Chr. 30, 16).

A miracle performed for the Israelites in the desert—a fire that comes forth from God and consumes the burnt offering on the altar during the inauguration of the tabernacle (Lev. 9, 24)—is reflected twice in the book of Chronicles; it is appended to two stories which, in the Chronicler's sources (the books of Samuel and Kings), are devoid of a miraculous element. God answers David with fire from heaven on the altar of burnt offerings in the story of Ornan's threshing floor (1 Chr. 21, 26), a story which preludes the complex of stories about the construction of the Temple in that book. The same miracle is repeated at the Temple's inauguration, the final stage of this process: "When Solomon finished praying, fire descended from heaven and consumed the burnt-offering and the sacrifices ... " (2 Chr. 7, 1). The two miracles thus supply a frame circumscribing this glorious chapter in the history of the House of David.

In the Second Temple period, the book of Psalms reaches its final form and is divided into five books (chapters 1-41; 42-72; 73-89; 90-106; 107-150). The division is marked by doxologies that conclude each book (chapter 150 serves as a doxology for the fifth book). The division seems to have existed as early as the days of Chronicles, in which the fourth doxology is cited (see 1 Chr. 16, 35-36). The impetus for the division into five seems to have been to liken David to Moses, to whom the five books of the Law are related: "You find whatever Moses did, David did ... As Moses gave five books of laws to Israel, so David gave five books of Psalms to Israel" (*The Midrash on Psalms*, trans. by W. G. Braude [New Haven 1959], p. 5).

Testaments und des antiken Judentums, Band 9], Frankfurt am Main 1989, pp. 471-472.

C

Our final and most striking example of a character whose life story is modelled after that of Moses is Jeroboam, son of Nebat. Jeroboam is presented by the Judean historiographer as the prototype of a sinner who is emulated by all the kings of the northern kingdom. Omri, for instance, "followed all the ways of Jeroboam son of Nebat and the sins which he committed and caused Israel to commit . . . " (1 Ki. 16, 26). We find the most striking example in the farewell address for the northern kingdom: "For Israel broke away from the House of David, and they made Jeroboam son of Nebat king. Jeroboam caused Israel to stray from the Lord and to commit great sins. and the Israelites persisted in all the sins which Jeroboam had committed; they did not depart from them. In the end, the Lord removed Israel from his presence . . . " (2 Ki. 17, 21-23). Despite this negative image, even Davidic historiographers do not succeed in blurring some of the Mosaic lines of Jeroboam's portrait: it appears that in the northern kingdom, which was founded by him, Jeroboam was considered a second Moses, a Moses *redivivus*. That Moses grew up in a royal palace enabled him to become a model for a king in the kingdom of Israel.[54]

Like Moses, who became the leader of the Israelite slaves in Egypt, so Jeroboam was the leader of the northern slaves who were enslaved to Solomon: " . . . and when Solomon saw that

---

54   The verse "Then became a king in Jeshurun . . . " (Dt. 33,5) is interpreted by S. Talmon as referring to Moses. See: "'In those Days There Was No מלך in Israel'—Judges 18-21," *King, Cult and Calendar in Ancient Israel*, Jerusalem 1986, p. 49. On Moses as a king see J. R. Porter, *Moses and Monarchy, A Study in the Biblical Tradition of Moses*, Oxford 1963; J. Pedersen, *Israel*, vols. 3-4, Copenhagen 1940, pp. 662-666. For post-biblical traditions presenting Moses as a king, see J. Heinemann, *Aggadah and its Development*, Jerusalem 1974, pp. 84-88 (Hebrew).

the young man was a capable worker, he appointed him over all the forced labor of the house of Joseph" (1 Ki. 11, 28). The word for "forced labor" (סבל) reminds us of the Egyptian bondage: "But the king of Egypt said to them, 'Moses and Aaron, why do you distract the people from their tasks? Get to your labors' " (לסבלותיכם; Ex. 5, 4). If Jeroboam is a Moses-type character, Solomon—for the house of Joseph—is of the Pharaoh-type.

a. The Israelites build "store cities (ערי מסכנות) for Pharaoh" (Ex. 1, 11) as they do also for Solomon, "This was the purpose of the forced labor. . . Solomon's store cities. . ." (1 Ki. 9, 15-19).

b. Pharaoh desires Moses' death: "When Pharaoh learned of the matter, he sought to kill Moses" (Ex. 2, 15); and Solomon that of Jeroboam: "Solomon sought to kill Jeroboam" (1 Ki. 11, 40).

c. Moses and Jeroboam escape, with the king in close pursuit: "But Moses fled from Pharaoh. He arrived in the land of Midian . . . " (Ex. 2, 15); " . . . but Jeroboam promptly fled to King Shishak of Egypt" (1 Ki. 11, 40).[55]

d. While Moses was born and bred in Egypt but was forced to flee to Midian, Jeroboam finds refuge in Egypt.

e. The situation of the Israelites in Egypt becomes more difficult with the death of Pharaoh: "A long time after that, the king of Egypt died. The Israelites groaned under the bondage and cried out, and their cry for help from the bondage rose up to God" (Ex. 2, 23). With the death of Solomon, the burden of the northern tribe increases. They are prepared to serve his son, Rehoboam, if he lightens "the harsh labor and the heavy yoke which your father [Solomon] laid on us . . . " (1 Ki. 12, 4). Rehoboam, however, is too stubborn to accept their terms.

55 A literal repetition of Jeroboam's flight can be found in Jesus' birth story (Mat. 2, 14). According to the Aramaic Targum to Song of Songs 8, 11-12, the prophet Ahiyah also escapes to Egypt (following the story of Jer. 26, 20-21).

f. With the death of Pharaoh, Moses returns to Egypt—after God has appointed him for his mission (Ex. 4); Jeroboam also returns after Solomon's death: "Jeroboam son of Nebat heard of it while he was still in Egypt, for Jeroboam had fled from King Solomon and had settled in Egypt" (2 Chr. 10, 2; some of the ancient versions read: "So Jeroboam returned from Egypt"). "They sent for him, and Jeroboam and all the assembly of Israel came and spoke to Rehoboam . . . " (1 Ki. 12, 2-3). Jeroboam is also chosen by God for his mission, as the prophet Ahijah says: " . . . For thus said the Lord, the God of Israel: I am about to tear the kingdom out of Solomon's hands, and I will give you ten tribes . . . " (1 Ki. 11, 31).

g. Moses asks of Pharaoh: "Thus said the Lord, the God of Israel: Let My people go that they may celebrate a festival for Me in the wilderness" (Ex. 5, 1), while Jeroboam requests of Rehoboam to lighten the heavy yoke imposed by his father (1 Ki. 12, 4).

h. In both cases, the king makes the burden yet heavier: "That same day Pharaoh charged the taskmasters and foremen of the people, saying: 'You shall no longer provide the people with straw for making bricks as heretofore; let them go and gather straw for themselves. But impose upon them the same quota of bricks as they have been making heretofore; do not reduce it, for they are shirkers; that is why they cry, "Let us go and sacrifice to our God!" Let heavier work be laid upon the men' " (Ex. 5, 6-9); "He spoke to them in accordance with the advice of the young men, and said, 'My father made your yoke heavy, but I will add to your yoke; my father flogged you with whips, but I will flog you with scorpions' " (1 Ki. 12, 14).

A clear example of the resemblance between Jeroboam's life story and the Exodus traditions is the king's fashioning of two golden calves, in Bethel and in Dan (1 Ki. 12, 28-30), an act considered by the Judean historiographer as the epitome of his sins. Aberbach and Smolar have already enumerated the resemblances between the story of the golden calf made in the desert (Ex. 32) and the Jeroboam tradition;[56] let us review their main points:

a. The act itself of molding the calves is common to both stories; note the term "a molten calf" (עגל מסכה; Ex. 32, 4, 8; Dt. 9, 12, 16; 1 Ki. 14, 9; 2 Ki. 17, 16).

b. Identical exclamations mark the completion of their making: "This is your God, O Israel, who brought you out of the land of Egypt" (Ex. 32, 4); "This is your God, O Israel, who brought you out of the land of Egypt" (1 Ki. 12, 28).

c. An altar is built next to the calf, and a festival (Ex. 32, 5; 1 Ki. 12, 32) and sacrifices (Ex. 32, 6; 1 Ki. 12, 32) follow.

d. Like Aaron, Jeroboam also serves as a priest (Ex. 32, 2-6; 1 Ki. 12, 33; 13, 1).

The similarity between the two golden calf stories was obvious to the Rabbis; consider for example: "R. Oshaia said: Until Jeroboam, Israel imbibed [a sinful disposition] from one calf; but from him onwards, from two or three calves" (BT *Sanhedrin* 102a, trans. J. Schachter and I. Epstein, London 1969).

Jeroboam's fashioning of the golden calves is certainly not a revolutionary act: his restoration of worship in the old and famous cultic sites of Bethel and Dan reflects the same intention to restore the traditional cult of the calves. It was clear to him and to his people that there was nothing forbidden about the calves; otherwise, he would not have succeeded in turning their hearts away from Jerusalem and its cult and attracting them to worship God in Bethel and Dan. We may conclude, then, that the calves were an old and respected element in the religion and cult of the northern tribes, an element deeply rooted in the Exodus traditions. But the ancient calf tradition told by the people of the North was undoubtedly very different from Exodus 32. That chapter is a tendentious and polemical Judean narrative which opposes the calf cult of the

56   M. Aberbach and L. Smolar, "Aaron, Jeroboam and the Golden Calves," *JBL* 86 (1967), pp. 129-140.

North[57] and seeks to defame it. This story indeed admits the antiquity of the calf tradition, going back to the days of the Exodus, but presents it as a heinous sin. In the North, on the other hand, the calves were considered a legitimate object of divine worship honoring the God of Israel. They did not identify the calf with God, but rather considered it a pedestal on which the invisible God stands; the calf served the same function that the cherubs served in Jerusalem.[58]

In the Exodus story, Aaron is the sinner while Moses is righteous, yet the possibility exists that in the northern tradition it was Moses who built the calf. A tradition that associates Moses with the priesthood, linked to the temple of one of the calves, is preserved in Judges 18, 30: "The Danites set up the sculptured image for themselves; and Jonathan son of Gershon son of Manasseh and his descendents served as priests to the Danite tribe until the land went into exile."[59] In the Hebrew, Manasseh is written with a suspended נ (מנ̇שה), indicating an earlier reading of משה ("Moses"; cf. Ex. 2, 22). The reading משה is preserved in some Hebrew and Greek manuscripts and in the Vulgate (see n. 12).

The story of the inauguration of the altar at Bethel is also manifestly tendentious and polemical, presenting a negative miracle: "The altar broke apart and its ashes were spilled . . . " (1 Ki. 13, 5). This is a sign of God's dissatisfaction with the Bethel cult, in contrast to the positive miracle of the fire issuing from heaven and consuming the burnt offerings on the altar during the inauguration of the Tabernacle (Lev. 9, 23-24),[60] which indicated God's satisfaction with the altar and the cult.

---

57 Ibid., p. 136.
58 See *Biblical Encyclopaedia* 6, p. 75 (Hebrew).
59 For another hint of Moses' priesthood see Psalm 99, 6, and for his involvement in a cultic act see Exodus 24, 4-8. That his father-in-law is the "priest of Midian" strengthens this concept.
60 See also p. 86.

The resemblance between Jeroboam and Moses is reinforced in an addition to 1 Kings 12 preserved in the Septuagint, originally formulated in Hebrew:[61]

> Now there was a man of Mount Ephraim, a servant of Solomon, whose name was Jeroboam and his mother's name was Sarira. She was a harlot (cf. 11, 26) and Solomon appointed him an overseer over all the forced labor of the House of Joseph (cf. 11, 28) ... He had built the Millo with [the] forced labor of the House of Ephraim ... Solomon sought to put him to death (cf. 11, 40) and he was terrified and fled to Shishak, King of Egypt, and he remained with him until the death of Solomon (cf. 11, 40, and the story of David's escape to Achish [1 Sam. 27, 3]).[62] When Jeroboam heard in Egypt that Solomon was dead, he addressed Shishak, King of Egypt and said, "Give me leave to go to my own country." Shishak replied, "What do you request and I will give it to you." For Shishak had given Jeroboam for a wife Ano, an elder sister of his own wife Tahpenes. She was great among the king's daughters and had borne Jeroboam his son Abia. And Jeroboam said to Shishak, "Nevertheless, give me leave to go." So Jeroboam left Egypt ...

This duplicate tradition also has little sympathy for Jeroboam: it makes no mention of his father's identity, while portraying his mother as a harlot.[63] One cannot ignore the relationship between this tradition and the story of Jephthah: Jephthah is "the son of a harlot" (Jud. 11, 1) who also has to flee from his country, "So Jephthah fled from his brothers and settled in the Tob country ... " (vs. 3) and is then invited to return and rule over his people.

---

61   For the Hebrew reconstruction of the Greek addition, see. Z. Talshir, *The Duplicate Story of the Division of the Kingdom (LXX 3 Kingdoms XII 24a-z)*, Jerusalem 1989, pp.129-134 (Hebrew).
62   Ibid., p. 51.
63   Ibid., p. 169.

Despite the hostile adaptation of the duplicate tradition, we can still discern in it some of the original Mosaic lines of Jeroboam's characterization. Jeroboam asks Shishak to let him go to his own country, as did Moses request of Pharoah (see Ex. 4, 23; 5, 3; 7, 16, etc., and cf. Jacob's request of Laban in Gen. 30, 25), and Shishak tries to prevent him. The story also mentions family ties between Jeroboam and Shishak that recall the relations of Moses with Pharaoh—his being brought up in the ruler's house as the adopted son of Pharaoh's daughter.

Before we jump to conclusions about the nature of the duplicate tradition and its relation to early northern traditions, we must investigate the relationship between the duplicate tradition and another story that bears much resemblance to it, the account of Hadad the Edomite in 1 Kings 11, 14-22, a story which follows the Exodus pattern as well:

Jeroboam's duplicate tradition *(Septuagint to 1 Kings 12)*	*The Hadad story* *(1 Kings 11, 14-22)*
When Jeroboam heard in Egypt that Solomon was dead,	When Hadad heard in Egypt that David had been laid to rest with his fathers and that Joab the army commander was dead,
he addressed Shishak, King of Egypt and said,	Hadad said to Pharaoh
"Give me leave to go to my own country."	"Give me leave to go to my own country" (vs. 21).
Shishak replied,	Pharaoh replied,
"What do you request and I will give it to you."	"What do you lack with me, that you want to go to your own country?" (vs. 22a).
For Shishak had given Jeroboam for a wife Ano an elder	. . . and gave him his sister-in-law, the sister of Queen

93

sister of his own wife Tahpenes.	Tahpenes, as wife (vs. 19).
She was great among the king's daughters	
and bore Jeroboam his son Abia,	The sister of Tahpenes bore him a son, Genubath.
	Tahpenes weaned him in Pharaoh's palace (vs. 20). . .
And Jeroboam said to Shishak	. . . But he said
"Nevertheless, give me leave to go."	"Nevertheless, give me leave to go" (vs. 22b).
So Jeroboam left Egypt.	

There are more Exodus-type elements in the Hadad story than in the Jeroboam duplicate tradition:

a. The reason for Hadad's escape is that every Edomite male was killed by Joab (1 Ki. 11, 16), an element paralleled in Exodus 1, 16-22.

b. The Hadad story mentions a certain relationship to Midian—"Setting out from Midian" (vs. 18)—a country which plays an important role in Moses' escape from Pharaoh (Ex. 2, 15*ff*.). "Paran" (vs. 18) is also mentioned in the Exodus narratives (Nu. 10, 12 etc.).

c. " . . . assigned a food allowance to him" (vs. 18)— Pharaoh's care for Hadad's nourishment finds its parallel in the story of the children of Israel in Egypt: "Joseph sustained his father and his brothers, and all his father's household with bread, down to the little ones" (Gen. 47, 12). In the Syriac translation to 1 Kings 11, 18, the words " . . . assigned a food allowance to him" are replaced with the words "Stay with me," which also appear in another story following the Exodus pattern, the story of Jacob in Haran: "Laban said, 'Better that I give her to you than that I should give her to an outsider. Stay with me" (Gen. 29, 19).

94

d. "... and granted him a land" (11, 18) is a clear resemblance to Pharaoh's giving the land of Goshen to the Israelites (see for instance Gen. 47, 11).

e. In 1 Kings 11, 19 we read, "Pharaoh took a great liking to Hadad," compared with Genesis 39, 21: "The Lord was with Joseph: He extended kindness to him and disposed the chief jailer favorably toward him."

f. It is not impossible that the name of Hadad's son, Genubath (גנבת; vs. 20), derived from the Hebrew root גנ"ב, "to steal," is also borrowed from the Exodus storehouse of motifs: consider Joseph's words: "For in truth I was stolen (גנב גנבתי) from the land of the Hebrews" (Gen. 40, 15).

Further assimilation between Hadad's story and the Exodus is engendered by Josephus Flavius who expands the description of Hadad's requests from Shishak to let him go: "... and when he was often troublesome to him, and entreated him to dismiss him, he did not then do it" (Ant., 8, 7, 6).

The most essential question, indeed, is how the similarity between the story of Hadad and the Jeroboam duplicate tradition was created. A second, related question concerns why Hadad is worthy of becoming the hero of an Exodus tradition (as opposed to another adversary of Solomon, Rezon son of Eliada [11, 23-25]). According to Talshir, the Jeroboam duplicate tradition is built from fragments of traditions borrowed from 1 Kings 11, 1 Kings 12 and 1 Kings 14,[64] including the Hadad story; she thinks it illogical to suppose that elements from a Jeroboam story were "stolen" to create a tradition about a minor character like Hadad.[65]

The process that actually took place seems to be precisely the opposite of what Talshir describes: I believe a direct relationship exists between the two stories, but the direction of borrowing was indeed from Jeroboam to Hadad: some Judean writers, not approving of the Mosaic lines of Jeroboam's image,

64 Ibid., p. 155.
65 Ibid., p. 173-174.

95

attempted to reduce the resemblances between the traditions. One of the ways they accomplished this was to transfer a tradition from one figure to another—from Jeroboam to the minor character of Hadad. This phenomenon is not foreign to us. The problematic birth tradition of Jacob and Esau, according to which Jacob supplants his brother already in their mother's womb (see Ho. 12, 4), was likewise transferred to another set of twin brothers, Perez and Zerah (Gen. 38, 27-30).[66]

66 Some scholars have realized that Hosea refers to a different birth tradition, and not to that of Genesis 25, 26: H. Gunkel, *Genesis[7]*, Göttingen, 1966, p. 296; B. Luther, *Die Israeliten und ihre Nachbarstämme* (von E. Meyer mit Beiträgen von B. Luther), Halle 1906, p. 128. The Hosea tradition resembles the birth tradition of Perez and Zerah (Gen. 38, 27-30); see H. Gressmann, *Die älteste Geschichtsschreibung und Prophetie Israels*, Göttingen 1910, p. 375. In Genesis 38 the brother expected to emerge second succeeds in preceding his brother and becomes the first-born. Since a tradition about a struggle between the two brothers ending with Jacob's deceitful victory puts Jacob to shame, it was rejected by the writer of the Jacob cycle, who replaced it with another story that still alludes to Jacob's attempt to delay his brother's birth by holding his heel. The rejected tradition was transferred to other biblical characters: the complete erasure of such a popular story from the national consciousness would have been impossible. Instead, the recycled tradition lives on, but in a "safe" form. The relationship between the two birth stories—one which rejected the original tradition and the other which adopted it—is indisputable; the sentence "there were twins in her womb" appears in both of them (Gen. 25, 24; 38, 27).
The writer of the Jacob cycle postpones the birth tradition to a period two generations later than Jacob and Esau. According to Genesis 38, Perez and Zerah are Jacob's grandchildren, Judah's sons from Tamar; but Zerah is also the name of Esau's grandchild, the son of Reuel (Gen. 36, 17; 1 Chr. 1, 37). Moreover, "Zerah" (זר"ח), means "to shine" in Hebrew, while the crimson thread (שני) tied onto Zerah's wrist may originally have served as an explanation for Edom's name (אדום), since the words שני and אדום (=red) are synonymous: "Be your sins like crimson

The transfer of the tradition from Jeroboam to Hadad did not completely erase the memory of the Jeroboam-Moses story. The original tradition found its way to a manuscript which became the Greek translator's *Vorlage*. Despite the tendency in the duplicate tradition to dim Jeroboam's glory by presenting his mother as a prostitute, the Greek translation still preserves the admiration of the northern kingdom for Jeroboam: for the people of the northern kingdom, Jeroboam was indeed the founder of the state, a second Moses who liberated them from the burden of the second Pharaoh, the king of Judah.

In light of the popularity of the Exodus traditions in the northern kingdom,[67] it is not surprising that the original nature of the Jeroboam tradition succeeded in emerging, despite the hostile curtaining, and helps us reconstruct the northern portrait of Jeroboam.

D

In this chapter, we have seen the expansiveness of the biblical Exodus tradition. Its presence fills the whole Bible, from the Genesis stories to the history of the Jews in exile in the book of Esther, and even to the redemption and return to their land, including the declaration of Cyrus in the book of Ezra. The inescapable dominance of the Exodus tradition over the entire Bible finds geographical expression as well—the "W" pattern which begins with Abraham leaving Haran, and ends

---

(כשנים) . . . Be they red (יאדימו) as dyed wool . . . " (Isa. 1, 18). The obvious link between Edom and Zerah stands behind the verse: "He [the Lord] shone up (זרח) from Seir" (another name of Esau-Edom; Dt. 33, 2). Despite the rejection of the original deceit tradition from the official, authoritative version of Jacob's birth story, it nonetheless remained alive, finding expression in the words of the prophets who fault the people of Israel for behaving like their father, Jacob (Isa. 48, 8; Jer. 9, 3-5; 17, 9).

67   See Hoffmann (n. 1), especially pp. 169-173, 181-184.

with the Babylonian exile. Moreover, we have seen some late manifestations of the Exodus pattern, as in the incident of "Remove your sandals from your feet" (Jos. 5, 13-15), with echoes in the book of Ruth and in the presentation of David in the book of Chronicles.

Moses, the leader of Israel during the Exodus, whose character is comprised of prophetic, priestly and even royal elements, casts a preeminent shadow over many biblical figures who were fashioned in his image: his disciple-successor Joshua; Gideon, the founder of a cult, a leader and almost-king; David, a true king, sire of a royal line and of the Jerusalem cult; yet another king, founder of a state and cult, who also serves as priest and liberates his people from the Judean bondage, Jeroboam; and two prophets, Elijah and his successor, Elisha. In general, the assimilation to Moses flatters the characters whose traditions imitate his biography, yet the comparison sometimes emphasizes the differences between Moses and his successors, as with Joshua and his spies (Jos. 2) and Elijah at Horeb (1 Ki. 19). Some of the original lines of the Mosaic biography were deliberately blurred and even concealed because they did not correspond with the concepts held by the biblical historiographers, such as the traditions concerning his kingship and priesthood, and the story of Moses' ascent to heaven. Echoes of these hidden traditions found their way to other biographies which were formed after the mold of Moses: Jeroboam's kingship and priesthood, and Elijah's ascent. Although none of these figures carry Moses' name, they are nonetheless clothed in the Mosaic paradigm, and walk in his footsteps.

"There is a People that Dwells Apart . . . "
The Ideal of Separatism

A

"In the Beginning"—Rabbi Isaac said: The Torah which is the Law book of Israel should have commenced with the verse (Ex. 12, 1) "This month shall be unto you the first of months," which is the first commandment given to Israel. What is the reason, then, that it commences with the account of the Creation? Because of the thought expressed in the text (Ps. 111, 6): "He declared to His people the strength of His works (i.e., He gave an account of the work of creation), in order that He might give them the heritage of the nations." For should the peoples of the world say to Israel, "You are robbers, because you took by force the lands of the seven nations of Canaan," Israel may reply to them, "All the earth belongs to the Holy One, blessed be He; He created it and gave it to whom He pleased. When He willed He gave it to them, and when he willed, He took it from them and gave it to us." [The first words of Rashi's commentary on the Torah][1]

Let us focus not on Rashi's polemic tendency, which involves the claim for Israel's right over the land, but on the alternative openings he suggests for the Torah. The question is raised why the Pentateuch, the history of the Israelite nation,

---

1   For the midrashic sources for Rashi's statement see H. D. Shevel's edition of Rashi's Commentary to the Torah, Jerusalem 1982, p. 1 (Hebrew).

begins with the Creation instead of with the Exodus—the Exodus representing a rebirth, the creation of the people of Israel with whom the laws are connected. Since the Creation, no event has measured in magnificence with God's choosing Israel. This conviction finds expression in the Exodus: "You have but to inquire about bygone ages that came before you, ever since God created man on earth, from one end of heaven to the other: has anything as grand as this ever happened, or has its like ever been known? Has any people heard the voice of a God speaking out of a fire as you have, and survived? Or has any god ventured to go and take for himself one nation from the midst of another by prodigious acts, by signs and portents, by war . . . as the Lord your God did for you in Egypt before your very eyes?" (Dt. 4, 32-34).

The same two events, the Creation and the Exodus, are named as the two reasons behind the commandment regarding the Sabbath: in the version of the commandments found in Exodus, the Sabbath is modelled on the story of Creation: "For in six days the Lord made heaven and earth . . . and He rested on the seventh day; therefore the Lord blessed the Sabbath day and hallowed it" (20, 11; cf. Gen. 2, 1-3; Ex. 31, 17).[2] In the Deuteronomy edition of the commandments, the reasoning is borrowed from the world of the Exodus: "Remember that you were a slave in the land of Egypt and the Lord your God freed you from there with a mighty hand and an outstretched arm; therefore the Lord your God has commanded you to observe the Sabbath day" (5, 15).

In Psalm 136, which enumerates God's mighty deeds and salvations, the poet passes directly from the Creation to the Exodus: "Who made the heavens with wisdom . . . Who spread the earth over the water . . . Who made the great lights . . . The sun to dominate the day . . . the moon and the stars to dominate the night . . . Who struck Egypt through the first-born . . . and brought Israel out of their midst . . . with a

---

2   All three belong to the priestly document of the Pentateuch.

100

strong hand and outstretched arm ... Who split apart the Sea of Reeds ... and made Israel pass through it ... Who hurled Pharaoh and his army into the Sea of Reeds ... " (vss. 5-15; cf. Ps. 135, 6-9).

It seems that these two monumental events were also originally associated in the opening of another historical review: Samuel's speech in 1 Samuel 12. The text, however, has become corrupted: "The Lord who made (עשה) Moses and Aaron and who brought your fathers out of the land of Egypt" (vs. 6). Commentators unanimously find it difficult to explain the meaning of the verb עשה in this context, while the mention of Moses and Aaron is also premature, as the speaker reaches them later in his review, in verse 8. I believe the original reading mentioned the two greatest events in the world's and Israel's history: "The Lord *who made* (created) *heaven and earth* and who brought your fathers out of the land of Egypt ... "—a reading we might compare with Nehemiah 9, 6: "You alone are the Lord, *you made the heavens*, the highest heavens, and all their host, *the earth* and everything upon it ... " The verse was corrupted when the word "heavens" (שמים) was replaced by the graphically similar word "Moses" (משה), and the word "the earth" (הארץ) was likewise replaced by "Aaron" (אהרן). The text may have been corrupted by a copyist who was influenced by the continuation of the verse, which speaks of the Exodus, and by the reference to Moses and Aaron in verse 8.

The parting of the Sea of Reeds—the greatest miracle of the Exodus—is similar both in nature and language to the presentation of the creation in the Canaanite epic of the sea's rebellion. Echoes of God's primeval war with the sea are numerous in the Bible. Cassuto, who gathers all the biblical references to the epic and reconstructs it,[3] writes: " ... in the Song of the

---

3 U. Cassuto, "The Israelite Epic," in *Biblical and Oriental Studies* (trans. I. Abrahams), Jerusalem 1975, vol. 1, pp. 69-109.

Sea, what happened to the children of Israel at the parting of the Sea of Reeds is described in the words, expressions and images that were commonly used in the tradition in relation to the suppression of the proud rising of the Sea during the six days of Creation."[4] The relationship between this creation epic and the Exodus was later emphasized by Loewenstamm[5] and Fenton,[6] who were well aware of the historicization process of the primeval myth.[7] Interestingly, the Canaanite epic mentions both the parting of a sea and a river, and its biblical echoes are discernable in Isaiah 11, 15, Nahum 1, 4 and Job 14, 11. The biblical tradition of the Exodus is framed between two acts of parting: the parting of the Sea of Reeds, marking the beginning of the journey, and the parting of the Jordan river, marking the end of the Israelite wandering and the entrance into the promised land (Jos. 3-4).[8] Of all the expressions linking the epic to the crossing of the sea in Exodus, let us consider only the root גע"ר ("rebuke"). In the creation tradition we find: "They [the waters] fled at Your blast (גערתך), rushed away at the sound of Your thunder" (Ps. 104, 7); while we find in the Exodus: "He sent his blast (ויגער) against the Sea of Reeds; it became dry" (Ps. 106, 9). We also find this root in other echoes of the myth: "He rebukes (גוער) the sea and dries it up, and he makes the rivers fail" (Na. 1, 4); " . . . Is my arm, then, too short to rescue, Have I not the power to save? With a mere rebuke I dry up the sea, and turn rivers into desert . . ." (Isa. 50, 2; see also 2 Sam. 22, 16 = Ps. 18, 16).[9]

---

4   Ibid., p. 75.
5   S. E. Loewenstamm, *The Tradition of the Exodus in its Development*, Jerusalem 1965, pp. 115-117 (Hebrew).
6   T. Fenton, "Differing Approaches to the Theomachy Myth in *presented to S. E. Loewenstamm*, ed. Y. Avishur and J. Blau, Jerusalem 1978 (Hebrew section), pp. 337-381.
7   See also F. M. Cross, *Canaanite Myth and Hebrew Epic*, Cambridge Mass. and London 1976, p. 143.
8   Fenton, p. 365.
9   See also Fenton, p. 350.

Scenarios of the future redemption of Israel also combine echoes of the creation myth with motifs borrowed from the Exodus: "The Lord will dry up the tongue of the Egyptian sea. He will raise His hand over the river with the might of His wind and break it into seven wadis, so that it can be trodden dry-shod. Thus there shall be a highway for the other part of His People out of Assyria, such as there was for Israel when it left the land of Egypt" (Isa. 11, 15-16); "Awake, awake, clothe yourself with splendor, O arm of the Lord! Awake as in days of old, As in former ages! It was you that hacked Rahab in pieces, that pierced the Dragon. It was you that dried up the Sea, the waters of the great deep. That made the abysses of the Sea a road the redeemed might walk. So let the ransomed of the Lord return, and come with shouting to Zion, Crowned with joy everlasting. Let them attain joy and gladness, While sorrow and sighing flee" (Isa. 51, 9-11).

The future redemption is modelled in the form of the Exodus also in Isaiah 43, 16-21. God presents his people as his creation: "The people I created for Myself" (vs. 21). Similarly, in the first verse of the chapter we find: "But now thus said the Lord, Who created you (בראך), O Jacob, Who formed you (יצרך), O Israel," expressions typical to the story of the creation of man (see Gen. 1, 27; 2, 7).[10]

In the narrative we find clear links to the traditions of the world's primeval history found in the book of Genesis (Gen. 1-11). For example, in the story of Moses' birth we read, "She saw how good he was" (Ex. 2, 2), which we compare with the creation story: "God saw that the light was good" (Gen. 1, 4; cf. also vss. 10, 12, 18, 21, 31). The rabbis took note of this kinship:

> "And when she saw him that he was good" (Ex. 2, 2) . . . and the Sages declare, At the time when Moses was born, the whole house was filled with light—it is written

10   For more references about Israel as created by God, see, for example, Dt. 32, 6; Mal. 2, 10; Ps. 102, 19.

here, "And when she saw him that he was good," and elsewhere it is written, "And God saw the light that it was good" (Gen. 1, 4). [BT *Sotah*, 12a]

The birth of Moses is also associated with another act of deliverance from water known to us from the primeval history, the flood story. Noah was rescued in a תבה, an "ark" (Gen. 6, 14). The single other appearance of this word in the Bible is in Exodus 2, 3, the "wicker basket" in which Moses' mother saves her infant: "When she could hide him no longer, she got a wicker basket for him . . ."! Noah is commanded, "and cover it inside and out with pitch" (Gen. 6, 14), as does Moses' mother: " . . . and [she] caulked it with bitumen and pitch" (Ex. 2, 3). Just as all the wicked meet their death in the flood, so the Egyptians meet theirs in the Sea of Reeds.

A multitude of common expressions link the flood story to the tradition of the parting of the Sea narrated in Exodus 14-15 and other biblical sources. Some examples: "the great deep" (תהום) appears in Genesis 7, 11; 8, 2; Exodus 15, 5, 8; Isaiah 51, 10; "to split" (בק"ע) in Genesis 7, 11; Ex. 14, 16, 21; Psalms 78, 15, etc.; "the waters turning back" (וישובו המים) in Genesis 8, 3; Exodus 14, 26, 28; "to cover" (כסה) in Genesis 7, 19, 20; Exodus 15, 10; Joshua 24, 7; Psalm 78, 53; "dry land" (חרבה) in Genesis 7, 22; Exodus 14, 21.

The Eden tradition is associated with the Exodus story as well: in Genesis 13, 10 the narrator compares the fruitfulness of Egypt to that of the garden of Eden: "Lot looked about him and saw how well watered was the whole plain of the Jordan . . . like the garden of the Lord, like the land of Egypt." The children of Israel are driven out of Egypt, "He shall drive them (יגרשם) from his land" (Ex. 6, 1; see also 12, 39); the Bible here employs the same verb as that in the expulsion of Adam from the garden: "He drove the man out . . ." (Gen. 3, 24). Moreover, a contrasting symmetry also exists between the two stories: man was expelled from the Garden of Eden into a world of hard labor, while the expulsion from Egypt freed the Israelites from their back-breaking work.

The creation of the people of Israel, the Exodus, took place at the beginning of the year: "The Lord said to Moses and Aaron in the land of Egypt: This month shall mark for you the beginning of the months; it shall be the first of the months of the year for you . . ." (Ex. 12, 1-2). In Jewish tradition, the creation of the world is similarly attributed to the beginning of the year, Rosh Hashanah, counting from either the month of Tishri or the month of Nissan:

> It has been taught: R. Eliezer says: In Tishri the world was created . . . In Nissan they were redeemed and in Nissan they will be redeemed in the time to come. R. Joshua says: In Nissan the world was created . . . on New Year the bondage of our ancestors ceased in Egypt; and in Nissan they will be redeemed in time to come. [BT *Rosh Hashanah* 10b-11a][11]

The Exodus, like the creation of the world, marks the beginning of something utterly new, unlike anything in the world's past or future, a beginning which emphasizes the uniqueness of the people of Israel and the attitude of the Creator toward them.

B

The created people, God's chosen nation, must do something in return for this favor; children are to be told of the Exodus miracle in order to strengthen their faith: " . . . And that you may recount in the hearing of your sons and of your sons' sons how I made a mockery of the Egyptians and how I displayed my signs among them—in order that you may know I am the

---

11 We find parallels to this in *Genesis Rabbah* 22, 4; *Leviticus Rabbah* 29, 1; *Pirke de-Rabbi Eliezer*, ch. 8.

Lord" (Ex. 10, 2). Likewise we read in the words of the historical psalm, which awakens the people to observe the law:

> Give ear, my people, to my teaching, turn your ear to what I say . . . things we have heard and known, that our fathers have told us. We will not withhold them from their children, telling the coming generation the praises of the Lord and His might, and the wonders He performed. He established a decree in Jacob, ordained a teaching in Israel, charging our fathers to make them known to their children, that a future generation might know—children yet to be born—and in turn tell their children that they might put their confidence in God, and not forget God's great deeds, but observe His commandments, and not be like their fathers, a wayward and defiant generation, a generation whose heart was inconstant, whose spirit was not true to God (Ps. 78, 2-8).

Unaccompanied by a permanent obligation, a story might not achieve its goal. The yearly Passover sacrifice is thus imposed in order to arouse the curiosity of the children who will ask, "What do you mean by this rite?" (Ex. 12, 26); and the father will answer: "It is the Passover sacrifice to the Lord, because He passed over the houses of the Israelites in Egypt when He smote the Egyptians, but saved our houses" (vs. 27). The obligation to eat unleavened bread reinforces the same idea: "And you shall explain to your son on that day, 'It is because of what the Lord did for me when I went free from Egypt' . . . in order that the teaching of the Lord may be in your mouth—that with a mighty hand the Lord freed you from Egypt. You shall keep this institution at its set time from year to year" (13, 8-10).

In the book of Deuteronomy, the questions posed by the sons apply to all the commandments that evidence God's glory:

> When, in time to come, your sons ask you, "What mean the decrees, laws and rules that the Lord our God has enjoined upon you?" you shall say to your sons, "We were slaves to Pharaoh in Egypt and the Lord freed us from Egypt with a

mighty hand. The Lord wrought before our eyes marvelous and destructive signs and portents in Egypt, against Pharaoh and all his household, and us He freed from there, that He might take us and give us the land that He had promised on oath to our fathers. Then the Lord commanded us to observe all these laws, to revere the Lord our God . . . " (6, 20-24).

Ibn Ezra summarizes these verses briefly and aptly: "God redeemed us from the house of bondage and did us this favor, so we are obliged to fear His name."[12]

The first commandment (according to the traditional division of the ten commandments) is, in fact, deliberately nothing more than a declaration; it is the authority behind the mandate to observe the laws: "I the Lord am your God who brought you out of the land of Egypt, the house of bondage" (Ex. 20, 2 = Dt. 5, 6).[13]

When a person brings the first fruits of his soil to the Temple, he is obliged to make a declaration: to give expression to the "credo" which associates the law of *bikkurim* with God's grace, continuously present since the Exodus:

> . . . My father was a fugitive Aramean. He went down to Egypt with meager numbers and sojourned there; but there he became a great and very populous nation. The Egyptians dealt harshly with us and oppressed us; they imposed heavy labor upon us. We cried to the Lord, the God of our fathers, and the Lord heard our plea and saw our plight, our misery and our oppression. The Lord freed us from Egypt by a mighty hand, by an outstretched arm and awesome power, and by signs and portents. He brought us

12 For more relationships between the Exodus miracle and the authority behind the law in the book of Deuteronomy, see Dt. 11, 2-9; 29, 24.

13 For the echoes of this commandment in biblical literature see, for instance, Ex. 6, 7; 29, 46; 32, 4; Lev. 19, 36; 22, 33; 25, 38, 55; 26, 13, 45; Dt. 6, 12; 8, 14; 13, 6, 11; 20, 1; Jos. 24, 17; 1 Ki. 9, 9; 12, 28; 2 Ki. 17, 36; Ho. 12, 10; 13, 4; Ps. 81, 10-11; Neh. 9, 18.

Chapter Three

to this place and gave us this land, a land flowing with milk and honey. Wherefore I now bring the first fruits of the soil which You, O Lord, have given me ... (Dt. 26, 5-10)

No one can simply thank God for the fertility of the land without drawing the historical connection to the primal cause, God's tremendous grace, the Exodus. Only God's providence, which is so manifest in the history of Israel, distinguishes between Him and the Baalim to whom other nations attribute fertility (see for example Ho. 2, 4-15).

Many individual laws also derive their authority from the Exodus. Among others we find: "You shall not wrong a stranger or oppress him, for you were strangers in the land of Egypt" (Ex. 22, 20; cf. 23, 9; as well as Lev. 19, 34: "The stranger who resides with you shall be to you as one of your citizens; you shall love him as yourself, for you were strangers in the land of Egypt"); and the Hebrew slave law in its Deuteronomy version: "Bear in mind that you were slaves in the land of Egypt and the Lord your God redeemed you; therefore I enjoin this commandment upon you today" (15, 15; cf. Lev. 25, 42). Such arguments are naturally more prevalent in the cultic realm, in laws directly related to the Exodus: the Passover sacrifice and the feast of Unleavened Bread (except for Ex. 12-13 also Ex. 23, 15; 34, 18; Dt. 16, 3) and the feast of Tabernacles (Lev. 23, 42-43).

The dependence of the laws on the Exodus explains why the history of the Israelites does not begin with the desert but rather with the Exodus of the Israelites from Egypt. Verses like Deuteronomy 32, 9-10, and Hosea 9, 10, represent exceptions to this view of history: "For the Lord's portion is His people, Jacob His own allotment, *He found him in the desert*, In an empty howling waste ... "; "*I found* Israel as grapes *in the desert*, your fathers seemed to Me like the first fig to ripen on a fig tree."

108

C

Like the Exodus miracles, the desert miracles that preceded the giving of the law were meant to prepare the Israelites for its observance. After the parting of the Sea of Reeds, the Israelites had barely reached the desert when they encountered their first difficulty: suffering three days of thirst, the people finally find a water source, only to discover that the water is bitter (Ex. 15, 22-23). The people grumble against Moses, who cries out to the Lord, and God provides him with a piece of wood with which he sweetens the water (vss. 24-25). The children of Israel, so recently saved from the Egyptians, have no patience or trust in God. They fail to rise to the trial before them, as the theological component of the story states: "There He made them a fixed rule and there He put them to the test" (vs. 25b). This component corresponds well with the first part of the story: when God indicates to Moses how to sweeten the water, the verb used is not "showed" (וייראהו) but "instructed" (וייורהו; vs. 25), a verb which is derived from the root יר"ה, the same root as in "Torah," (תורה; the Law). We read in the *Mekilta de-Rabbi Ishmael*: "R. Simeon b. Johai says: He showed him a teaching of the Torah. For it really says 'And the Lord taught him' (וייורהו) a tree: It is not written here 'And He showed him' (וייראהו) but 'And He taught him' (וייורהו) just as in the passages 'And he taught me (וירני) and said unto me . . . ' (Pr. 4, 4) (*Sidra Vayassa*, 1).[14]

Clearly, then, the purpose of the miracle was not to solve a problem, to overcome a difficulty caused by defective planning, but to examine Israel's faith in God and to train them in observing His laws: "He said, 'If you will heed the Lord your God diligently, doing what is upright in His sight, giving ear to His commandments and keeping all His laws, then I will

---

14 See M. Margaliot, "Marah (Exodus 15:22-27)," *Shnaton, An Annual for Biblical and Ancient Near Eastern Studies* 4 (1980), pp. 129-150, esp. p. 136 (Hebrew).

not bring upon you any of the diseases that I brought upon the Egyptians . . . '" (vs. 26). Additional proof that the thirst represents a test is found at the very end of the Marah story: "And they came to Elim, where there were twelve springs of water and seventy palm trees; and they encamped there beside the water" (vs. 27). Had God wanted to prevent a shortage of water, He would have brought them to Elim earlier! The miracle, however, had to occur: Israel lacked faith, and when they fail the test, God does not punish them but performs another miracle for them, hoping this time they will learn their lesson and realize He takes care of them and is aware of all their needs, requiring only that they observe all His laws.[15]

The test of thirst is immediately succeeded by a test of hunger. Once again, despite the last deliverance, the Israelites do not meet the challenge, and they begin complaining immediately: "In the wilderness, the whole Israelite community grumbled against Moses and Aaron. The Israelites said to them: 'If only we had died by the hand of the Lord in the land of Egypt, when we sat by the fleshpots, when we ate our fill of bread . . . ' " (16, 2-3). After the previous test, God made a statute to Israel (15, 25); this time He seeks to know if they will observe it: "And the Lord said to Moses, 'I will rain down bread for you from the sky, and the people shall go out and gather each day that day's portion—that I may thus test them, to see whether they will follow my instructions or not'" (16, 4). In the continuation of the story, God tests Israel with the observance of the Sabbath: gathering manna on the seventh day, the Sabbath, was forbidden since they had gathered enough for two days on the sixth day (vss. 22-26). And still, despite the awe-inspiring miracle of the double portion that fell on the sixth day and its perfect preservation—

15 On the concept of testing in the wilderness miracles, see J. Licht, *Testing in the Hebrew Scriptures and in Post-Biblical Judaism*, Jerusalem 1973, pp. 37-39 (Hebrew).

" . . . and it did not turn foul, and there were no maggots in it" (vs. 24)—some Israelites still violate the law: "Yet some of the people went out on the seventh day to gather, but they found nothing" (vs. 27). This violation arouses God's vehement reaction: "How long will you men refuse to obey my commandments and my teachings?" (vs. 28). An escalation is thus discernable from the Marah story to the manna story: the second time, the people fail the test even after the miracle has been performed.

The escalation continues with chapter 17, in which the one who was tested now tests: when the children of Israel again suffer from thirst they question their God. As soon as they encamp in Rephidim, without any hesitation (and the narrator studiously avoids telling us how serious the situation was), they complain: "'Give us water to drink,' . . . and Moses replied to them, 'Why do you quarrel with me? Why do you try the Lord?'" (vs. 2). In this case, the people's sin is eternalized in the site's name: "The place was named Massah and Meribah, because the Israelites quarreled and because they tried the Lord saying, 'Is the Lord present among us or not?' " (vs. 7).

D

The series of tests and miracles which express the Creator's providence over His chosen people is designed to prepare Israel for the giving of the Law. All the laws were given to Israel in the wilderness, in a cultural vacuum, far from any human habitation and any possible influence. Thus does the prophet Jeremiah characterize the desert: "They never asked themselves, 'Where is the Lord who brought us up from the land of Egypt, who led us through the wilderness, a land of deserts and pits, a land of drought and darkness, a land no man had traversed, where no human being had dwelt'" (2, 6).

The concept that the Israelite religion and its law is a unique phenomenon, unparalleled in any other human culture and incomparable to any other human act, necessitates the supposition that it is a heavenly creation: the Law in its entirety was given by God to Moses in the middle of nowhere, in the wilderness. All the laws are thus enclosed within a precise historiographic context: between the Exodus, which grants God the authority to demand observance of the law, and the entrance into Canaan, to which the Israelites come well equipped with their own culture, the heavenly law: the whole legal system they may need for their future life in Canaan. It is for this reason that, from the book of Joshua to the book of Kings, we find no evidence of any laws being given in the Land of Israel, and no leader or king plays the role of legislator.[16] Moreover, the kings themselves, like all other human beings, are subject to the laws given in the desert: "When he is seated on his royal throne, he [the King] shall have a copy of this Teaching written for him on a scroll by the levitical priests. Let it remain with him and let him read in it all his life, so that he may learn to revere the Lord his God, to observe faithfully every word of this teaching as well as these laws. Thus he will not act haughtily toward his fellows or deviate from the Instruction to the right or to the left . . . " (Dt. 17, 18-20).

We find only one exception, one law given by a king (and it was before he became a king), and even this example is dubious: following the soldiers' demand not to share the booty with those who remained with the baggage, David tells them: " . . . You must not do that, my brothers, in view of what the Lord has granted us, guarding us and delivering into our hands the band that attacked us. How can anyone agree with you on this matter? The share of those who remain with the baggage shall be the same as the share of those who go down

---

16   See R. Yaron, "The Evolution of Biblical Law," *La formazione del dritto nel Vicino Oriente Antico*, Rome 1988, pp. 90-93.

to battle; they shall share alike" (1 Sam. 30, 23-24). The narrative then announces: "So from that day on it was made a law for Israel, continuing to the present day" (vs. 25). This verse, which makes the story etiological, seems to be secondary—not because a similar law is well-known from the Pentateuch (Nu. 31, 25-27), but because David is surprised by the soldiers' demand: "How can anyone agree with you in this matter?" Sharing the booty between the warriors and those who remain behind must have been a well-established custom.[17]

Another law which appears to have been given in the land of Israel is found in the story about Joshua's covenant in Schechem (Jos. 24, 25). However, this whole chapter, in which no knowledge of the giving of the Law in the wilderness is attested, reflects a singular view found nowhere else in biblical historiography; this contention will be explored further below.[18]

Laws which were established following precedents are limited to the Pentateuch as well, while the decision is never one of a human court but always of God's judgement. Thus it is in the story about the man who gathered wood on the

---

17 On the secondary nature of etiological elements in biblical narrative, see I. L. Seeligmann, "Aetiological Elements in Biblical Historiography," *Zion* 26 (1961), pp. 153-157 (Hebrew). It seems that the interpolator was interested in making David a second Moses, see pp. 79-86.

18 The historiographic books also record rules made to commemorate certain events: " . . . so it became a custom (חק) in Israel for the maidens of Israel to go every year, for four days in the year, and chant dirges for the daughter of Jephthah the Gileadite" (Jud. 11, 39-40); "Jeremiah composed laments for Josiah which all the singers, male and female, recited in their laments for Josiah, as is done to this day; they became customary (לחק) in Israel . . . " (2 Ch. 35, 25; the context is similar to that of the story of the daughter of Jephthah!); "The Jews undertook and irrevocably obliged themselves and their descendants . . . to observe these two days in the manner prescribed and at the proper time each year . . . " (Est. 9, 27).

Sabbath: "He was placed in custody, for it had not been specified what should be done to him. Then the Lord said to Moses: The man shall be put to death; the whole community shall pelt him with stones outside the camp. So the whole community took him outside the camp and stoned him to death—as the Lord had commanded Moses" (Nu. 15, 34-36; see also Lev. 24, 10-23; Nu. 27, 1-11).

According to the Bible's view, the heavenly law given to Israel in the cultural vacuum of the wilderness will meet the needs of the future. No further legislation will be necessary, irregardless of changing sociological, economic or political conditions.

The desire to avoid even a semblance of any foreign cultural influence on the Israelite culture mandates the death, without leaving the desert, of the whole generation that came out of Egypt; only the generation born in the wilderness, who receives their law there, actually enters the land. Those who left Egypt, whose fear was aroused by the report of the spies about the land of Canaan, never reach Israel (Nu. 14, 21-23). Forty years, until the whole generation of fathers dies, their children must wander in the wilderness: "Your children who, you said, would be carried off—these will I allow to enter; they shall know the land that you have rejected. But your carcasses shall drop in this wilderness, while your children roam the wilderness for forty years . . . you shall bear your punishment for forty years, corresponding to the number of days— forty days—that you scouted the land; a year for each day . . . " (vss. 31-34; see also 32, 13; Jos. 5, 6; Ps. 95, 10). Only two men, Caleb and Joshua, the spies who did not speak ill of the country, are permitted to enter the land of Canaan (vss. 24, 30, 38).

Even the leaders—Moses, who gave the Law to Israel, Aaron and Miriam—must die in the wilderness. Moses will lead the people to the country's threshold and even view the land from a distance (Dt. 34, 1-3) but will not enter. According to Deuteronomy 1, 37, Moses is punished along with the whole generation who left Egypt for the sin of the spies. According to Numbers 20, 1-13, he and Aaron are punished for striking the rock in a desperate attempt to provide drink for the people rather than commanding it verbally to yield its water (see also 27, 14; Dt. 32, 51).[19] Before recounting her brothers' sin, the Bible reports Miriam's death (Nu. 20, 1), because she too cannot enter the land.

The continuity of generations and epochs is thus achieved by returning the remains of those who left Canaan, the dead Jacob and Joseph, to be buried there. The book of Genesis concludes with the burial of Jacob in his father's grave (49, 29-50, 14) and with Joseph's order to his brothers to bring his own bones to Canaan: "So Joseph made the sons of Israel swear . . . saying, 'When God has taken notice of you, you shall carry up my bones from here'" (vs. 25, and see Ex. 13, 19; Jos. 24, 32).[20]

The isolationist ideal which stands behind the tradition of giving the Law in the wilderness finds expression as well in earlier periods in the history of Israel: the patriarchs wander in the land, walking on the periphery, steering clear of highly populated areas and building some altars. Their main dealing is with God. They zealously avoid intermarriage with Canaanites (Gen. 24; see also 26, 34-35; 27, 46-28, 9) and their involvement with the local people is minimal: Genesis

---

19 On the reasons for Moses' death given in the Bible, see S. E. Loewenstamm, "The Death of Moses," in *Studies on the Testament of Abraham*, ed. G. W. E. Nickelsburg Jr., Montana 1976, pp. 185-217.

20 According to the *Testaments of the Twelve Patriarchs*, every son of Jacob commanded his own sons to carry up his bones from Egypt and to bury them in Hebron. The same tradition is documented in the midrash: "And whence do we know that they also carried up with them the bones of all the other founders of the tribes? From the expression 'Away hence with you' (Ex. 13, 19)" (*Mekilta de-Rabbi Ishmael, Sidra Beshallah*, trans. J. Z. Lauterbach, Philadelphia 1976, vol. 1, p. 181).

14 recalls only that Abraham had allies, Eshkol and Aner (vs. 13); the purchase of land obliges some negotiations with the local population (Gen. 23; 33, 18-20), while conflicts about water are also reported (21, 25-26; 26, 15-21). Occasionally, when the separatism of the patriarchs is not decisive enough, the episode ends badly—such as the story of Dinah who went out to visit the daughters of the land in Genesis 34, and the story of the marriage of Judah to a Canaanite woman in Genesis 38.

In Egypt as well, where the Israelites were transformed from a family to a people, they had their own isolated region, the land of Goshen. This isolation served both nations, as Joseph explains: "So when Pharaoh summons you and asks, 'What is your occupation?' you shall answer: 'Your servants have been breeders of livestock from the start until now, both we and our fathers'—so that you may stay in the land of Goshen. For all the shepherds are abhorrent to Egyptians" (Gen. 46, 33-34). Similarly, in the ten plagues narratives, the isolation of the Israelites evokes special comment. In the case of the wild beasts, for instance, we read: "But on that day I will set apart the land of Goshen, where my people dwell, so that no wild beasts shall be there, that you may know that I the Lord am in the midst of the land" (Ex. 8, 18; see also 9, 4, 6, 26; 10, 23). What is more, the Israelites are entrenched in hard labor and have no spare time or energy to absorb the Egyptian culture. The narrator is also very brief in recounting the history of the servitude period,[21] and the only memories the Israelites in the desert carry from Egypt are culinary ones: "If only we had died by the hand of the Lord in the land of Egypt, when we sat by the fleshpots, when we ate our fill of bread! . . . " (Ex. 16, 3; see also Nu. 16, 13).

The rabbis described well this separatist tendency: the effort of the Israelites to remain aloof from and untouched by the Egyptian culture:

21   See p. 17.

R. Hunna stated in the name of Bar Kappara: Israel was redeemed from Egypt on account of four things, viz. because they did not change their names, they did not change their language . . . They did not change their names—having gone down as Reuben and Simeon, and having come up as Reuben and Simeon. They did not call Judah 'Leon', nor Reuben 'Rufus' . . . They did not change their language as may be inferred from the fact that it is written elsewhere, "And there came one that had escaped, and told Abram the Hebrew" (Gen. 14, 13), while here it is written, "The God of the Hebrews hath met with us" (Ex. 3, 18) and it is also written, "It is my mouth that speaketh unto you" (Gen. 45, 12), which means that he spoke in Hebrew. [*Leviticus Rabbah* 32, 5 and parallels (London-N.Y. 1983, pp. 413-414)]

Nevertheless, some exceptions to this mainstream concept admittedly exist. According to the first-born plague story, the Israelites live among the Egyptians. They are so otherwise indistinguishable that they must mark their houses with blood in order not to be destroyed by the plague (12, 13, 21-23). Also God's promise to Moses seems not to assume the isolation of the Israelites: "And I will dispose the Egyptians favorably toward this people, so that when you go, you will not go away empty-handed. Each woman shall borrow from her neighbor and the lodger in her house objects of silver and gold and clothing" (3, 21-22; see also 11, 2; 12, 35-36). Furthermore, Moses was raised in Pharaoh's house (2, 10) and only on reaching adulthood does he venture out to join his kinfolk (vs. 11); yet we hear nothing about his education in his early years. A double reason explains his growing up in the house of Pharaoh's daughter. First, a person who is raised as a slave is incapable of becoming a leader and turning slaves into free men. Second, the narrative mocks Pharaoh, showing that his evil intent to kill all the Israelite boys was ironically frustrated: the boy who eventually ruined him was raised in his own home.

During Moses' lifetime, as well as throughout the wanderings in the desert, it was always clear that any contact made with gentiles would not lead to any cultural exchange between Israel and the other nations. Moses' father-in-law is the priest of Midian (Ex. 2, 16-22),[22] but the Bible emphasizes that his relationship with Moses left no cultural impact: Jethro first encountered his son-in-law in the wilderness and expressed his recognition of the greatness of the God of Israel: "Now I know that the Lord is greater than all gods" (18, 11); he aided Moses in organizing the court system, yet Moses sent him back to his own country (vs. 27) before the giving of the Law! What is more, the book of Deuteronomy is even critical of Jethro's contribution to the Israelite legal administration, and, completely ignoring his part, Moses attributes Jethro's reform to himself (1, 9-17). In another meeting with his father-in-law, Moses fails to convince him to join the Israelites. Jethro's final words are: "I will not go . . . but will return to my native land" (Nu. 10, 30), a statement which reminds us of God's words to Abraham, "Go forth from your native land and from your father's house" (Gen. 12, 1), thus calling our attention to the difference between the two. Moses wants his father-in-law to be the "eyes" of the Israelites, guiding them in the wilderness (Nu. 10, 31), but the juxtaposition with the coming verses testifies that they did not really need his assistance: "They marched from the mountain of the Lord a distance of three days. The Ark of the Covenant of the Lord traveled in front of them . . . to seek out a resting place for them" (vs. 33).[23]

The contributions of other gentiles, such as the prophet Balaam, are similarly devalued: earlier traditions praise

---

22 In some expressions of the Exodus pattern, the host gives his daughter to the fugitive slave; see p. 83 and pp. 92-94.

23 See M. Margaliot, "Hobab - Numbers 10:29-36," *Shnaton, An Annual for Biblical and Ancient Near Eastern Studies* 7-8 (1983-4), pp. 91-108 (Hebrew).

Balaam as a man of honor who would say nothing but what God told him, causing him to bless Israel. Later traditions mock him (the she-ass story, Nu. 22, 22-35) and even speak evil of him (Dt. 23, 5-6; Jos. 13, 22; Neh. 13, 2). The secondary elements in the story of the revenge of the Midianites for Baal-Peor in Numbers 31, 8b, 16 deserve our special attention.[24] According to the last verse, "Yet they are the very ones who, at the bidding of Balaam, induced the Israelites to trespass against the Lord in the matter of Peor," Balaam bears the guilt for the temptation of the Israelites by the daughters of Moab (Nu. 25, 1), as if his words, "No harm is in sight for Jacob, No woe in view for Israel" (23, 21), make clear that God's blessing to Israel is conditional, dependent on their righteousness and separatism. The temptation by the foreign women made them vulnerable. Pseudo-Philo aptly exposed the meaning of the juxtaposition of Numbers 24 and 25:

> And then Balaam said to [Balak], "Come and let us plan what you should do to them. Pick out the beautiful women who are among us and in Midian, and station them naked and adorned with gold and precious stones before them. And when they see them and lie with them, they will sin against their Lord and fall into your hands; for otherwise you cannot fight against them." [*Antiquities of the Bible* 18, 13-14, in *The Old Testament Pseudepigrapha*, ed. J. H. Charlesworth (Garden City-N.Y. 1985), vol. 2, p. 326][25]

The first meeting of the Israelites with gentiles after the Exodus occurs in the desert, in the war with the Amalekites (Ex. 17, 8-16). This war is a direct result of Israel's sin and a necessary punishment. The last words of the previous story, Massah and Meribah, "Is the Lord present among us or not?"

24 See my review of A. Rofé's *The Book of Balaam* (see n. 25) in *Kiryat Sefer* 54 (1979), p. 789 (Hebrew).

25 On the development of the Balaam traditions in the Bible and the transition from a positive to a negative approach, see A. Rofé, *The Book of Balaam (Numbers 22:2-24:25)*, Jerusalem 1979.

(Ex. 17, 7), were added in order to combine it with the war story that follows it: the war serves to prove God's presence to the sceptical nation. The question "Is the Lord present?" suits a military context; the Lord is present in the camp and delivers his people (see 1 Sam. 4, 3 and also Ex. 34, 9; Dt. 1, 42; Jos. 3, 5). This is the understanding in Numbers 14, 41-43 as well, which tells of another punishment earned by Israel—a war against the Amalekites—that is clearly related to our story: "But Moses said, 'Why do you transgress the Lord's command? This will not succeed. Do not go up, lest you be routed by your enemies, for the Lord is not in your midst. For the Amalekites and the Canaanites will be there to face you, and you will fall by the sword.' "[26] Because the doubting nation suggested two possibilities, "Is the Lord present . . . or not," the war was sent to supply the right answer. When Moses lifts his hand clasping the rod of God, Israel prevails; when he lowers his hand, the Amalekites prevail (vs. 11). The rabbis pointed out the relationship between the two adjacent stories:

> R. Levi said: What parable applies here to Israel? The parable of a man who had a son whom he placed on his shoulder and took to the market. There, when the son saw a desirable object, he said to his father, "Buy it for me," and his father bought for him what he wanted the first time he asked, the second time, and the third. But then, when the son saw someone whom he asked, "Have you seen my father?" the man said to his son: "You fool, you

26 It is possible that in the parallel version of the story (Dt. 1, 43-44) the enemy is the Amorites, because the hill country of the Amorites is mentioned in the very same chapter (vss. 19-20). In the Samaritan Pentateuch to Deuteronomy we find both the Amalekites and the Canaanites—a harmonization with the Numbers version. I do not exclude the possibility that the present text of Numbers mentions the Canaanites, who are sometimes identical with the Amorites, as a harmonization with Deuteronomy.

120

are astride my shoulder, whatever you wish I buy for you,
and yet you ask that man, 'Have you seen my father?'"
What did the father do then? He threw his son from his
shoulder, and a dog came and bit the son.

So, too, after Israel went out of Egypt, the Holy One, [like
a loving father], encompassed them with seven clouds of
glory, as is said "He compassed him about, He cared for
him" (Dt. 32, 10). They asked for manna: He gave it. For
quail: He gave them. After He gave all that they asked,
they proceeded to ruminate "Is the Lord among us, or not?"
(Ex. 17, 7). The Holy One said to them: You ruminate as to
My presence in your midst? As you live, I shall make you
aware of it. Here is a dog to bite you. And who was the
dog? Amalek, for the very next verse in Exodus says, "Then
came Amalek" (Ex. 17, 8). Hence "Remember . . . " (Dt. 25,
17)! [*Pesikta de-Rab Kahana* (Philadelphia 1975, p. 40)]

The Bible itself bears testimony to an awareness of the sig-
nificance of the juxtaposition: "Remember what Amalek did to
you on your journey, after you left Egypt, how he surprised you
on the march, and cut down all the stragglers in your rear,
when you were faint and weary and feared not God" (Dt. 25,
17-18). The last words—"and feared not God"—should be
understood as referring to the Israelites and not to the
Amalekites, as the Masorites and all subsequent commentators
have claimed. A sudden change of subject hardly makes sense,
and Amalek is not expected to fear God in any case. These
words, then, refer to Israel's behavior in the Massah and
Meribah incident, which justifies God's interference and punishment through the Amalekites.

E

The relationship discussed in section C between Israelite
separatism and the giving of the Law in the wilderness can
also be demonstrated indirectly in Joshua's historical review

121

in Joshua 24, an account which expresses a number of very unique traditions. Recognizing the exceptional nature of this chapter, it becomes necessary to distinguish between original elements of the speech and secondary elements which were added in order to harmonize it with well-known historical concepts and traditions. The survey begins with a declaration that idolatry was not foreign to Israel's ancestors: "In olden times, your forefathers [. . .] lived beyond the Euphrates and worshipped other gods" (vs. 2). The words I have left out, "Terah, father of Abraham and father of Nahor," are an addition which switches from the plural "your forefathers" to the singular "Terah";[27] the intent of the addition is to make it clear that Terah, but not his son, worshipped idols. This addition calls forth Laban's words to Jacob when they made their pact: "May the God of Abraham and the God of Nahor judge between us—their ancestral God" (Gen. 31, 53), where the last words are also an addition (they are absent in some Hebrew and Greek manuscripts). The intent here is to unify the two disparate deities, and to identify them with the God of Israel. The Samaritan Pentateuch and the Septuagint read ישפט ("judge") in the singular, to avoid any misunder-standing.

When Joshua reaches the Exodus in his account, the words "I sent Moses and Aaron" (ואשלח את משה ואת אהרן; vs. 5) are puzzling. They are indeed missing in the Septuagint where there is no room for Moses and Aaron, as it is God who, unassisted, saves the Israelites: "And I plagued Egypt . . . after which I freed you" (vs. 5). The addition in the Masoretic Text was borrowed from another historical survey, 1 Samuel 12, 8, by a reader who couldn't believe that Moses plays no role—not even being mentioned!—in this account of the Exodus.[28]

27 G. A. Cooke, *The Book of Joshua* (CB), Cambridge 1918, p. 214.
28 In the Bible there are many descriptions of the Exodus which do not mention Moses, such as the historical psalms 78 and 105 and the historical survey of Nehemiah 9—all of which express polemics against a Moses personality cult. Many miracles in

At the end of verse 5 and beginning of verse 6 there is a duplication: "After which I freed you; I freed your fathers." Different manuscripts of the Septuagint choose between the duplicate readings: Ms. Vaticanus leaves out the words "you; I freed" and reads "after which I freed your fathers," while Ms. Alexandrinus omits the words "I freed your fathers" and reads "I freed you"; the latter is most likely the original reading. The addition emphasizes that the generation of the fathers left Egypt, while Joshua addresses his speech in Schechem to the sons. Once again, some reader wanted to make certain that this speech would not contradict the common belief that the whole generation freed from Egypt indeed died in the desert (Nu. 14, 28-35).

The fathers' secondary stratum appears in the speech in other verses, from which it can easily be removed. In order to find the original of verse 6 we need only to change "and you came to the Sea. And the Egyptians pursued *your fathers*" to read "and you came to the Sea and the Egyptians pursued

which Moses, according to the prosaic-historiographical report of the Pentateuch, actively participates, are mentioned again in the Bible without any reference to Moses. The example of the parting of the Sea of Reeds will suffice to prove the point: according to Exodus 14 Moses assists God, a cooperation which totally disappears in the poetic version (Ex. 15; see also Jos. 2, 10; 4, 23; Ps. 66, 5-6; 114, 1-3; 106, 9-11; 136, 13-15). Psalm 77 is exceptional: it describes Israel's redemption by God with mythic overtones, including clear references to the parting of the sea without mentioning Moses (vss. 17-20). Toward the end of the psalm, Moses and Aaron are suddenly recalled in a secondary stratum: "You led your people like a flock in the care of Moses and Aaron" (vs. 21). This unexpected return to the picture of Moses and Aaron finds its parallel in the addition of the two brothers to Joshua's speech in Joshua 24, 5. The polemic against a Moses personality cult continues later in the Passover Haggadah, in which he is ignored completely. The concept of the Haggadah is: "'The Lord brought us out of Egypt'—not through an angel, not through a messenger, but the Holy One, blessed be He, He alone, in His glory . . . "

you"; in verse 7 only a slight change is necessary from *"They* cried out to the Lord, and He put darkness between you and the Egyptians" to *"You* cried . . . " Verse 17 contains another duplication: "For it was the Lord our God who brought us *and our fathers* out from the land of Egypt . . . and who wrought those wondrous signs before our very eyes . . . and guarded us all along the way that we traveled and among all the peoples through whose midst we passed." In fact, the Syriac version does not include the secondary element: "and our fathers."[29]

Another element in the speech, "After you had lived a long time in the wilderness" (vs. 7b), also seems to be secondary, as it contributes nothing to the argumentation. The addition, which is another attempt to harmonize the speech with common knowledge about the Exodus and which suits the concept of the fathers stratum, cuts the natural continuity of God's acts of salvation: "Your own eyes saw what I did to the Egyptians (vs. 7a[b]); I brought you to the land of the Amorites . . . " (vs. 8).

Joshua's historical survey sets the long list of God's acts of salvation against Israel's continuing idolatry, which was practiced not only beyond the Euphrates but in Egypt as well: "Now, therefore, revere the Lord and serve Him with undivided loyalty; put away the gods that your forefathers served beyond the Euphrates and in Egypt, and serve the Lord" (vs. 14). This marginal tradition about idolatry in Egypt is also known from Ezekiel 20, 7-8 (see also Dt. 29, 15-19).[30]

Thus, Joshua 24 does not share the separatism concept. The opposite is true: according to Joshua 24, the children of Israel take part in the local culture wherever they are; Israel has a continuous history of idolatry and only now, in Schechem, Joshua offers them various options to consider: either to

[29]   On the secondary nature of the fathers' stratum, see for instance Cooke (n. 27), pp. 216-218.

[30]   On the Israelites' idolatry in Egypt see M. Greenberg, *Ezekiel 1-20* (AB) Garden City, New York 1983, p. 365.

worship God or to cleave to the gods they used to worship beyond the Euphrates and in Egypt, and which they still worship (vs. 14), or even to adopt the gods of the country they have just entered (vs. 15). The people, grateful to God for the Exodus, choose to worship Him: "Far be it from us to forsake the Lord and serve other gods: For it was the Lord our God who brought us . . . from the land of Egypt" (vss. 16-17).

The absence of separatism and the continuity of idolatry according to Joshua 24 preclude the giving of the Law in the wilderness. Only in Schechem, with the decision to cleave to God and worship Him exclusively, can the Law be given. After the alien gods are put away (vs. 23) and after the Israelites declare, "We will serve the Lord our God and we will obey him" (vs. 24; compare the people's declaration after the giving of the Law in Ex. 24, 7), then Joshua can give the law to the children of Israel: "Joshua made a covenant for the people and he made a fixed rule for them (וישם לו חק ומשפט) at Schechem" (vs. 25). The terminology is similar to that used in another giving of law, by Moses, following the miracle of sweetening the water in Marah: "There he made them a fixed rule" (שם שם לו חק ומשפט; Ex. 15, 25).

The dominant separatist trend rejected the tradition that law was given within the land of Israel, in Schechem. That tradition, which might have been popular among the northern tribes, especially among the house of Joseph, is very logical. It is natural for a link to have been made between the law and a famous temple—a tangible monument commemorating the exact place where the law was given to Israel.[31]

31 A remarkable example of a polemic reflecting the tradition that the law was given in Schechem is found in Genesis 35 in Jacob's call to remove the alien gods, "Rid yourselves of the alien gods in your midst" (vs. 2b[a]; cf. Jos. 24, 23a), and their actual removal and burial: "They gave to Jacob all the alien gods that they had, and the rings that were in their ears, and Jacob buried them under the terebinth that was near Schechem" (vs. 4; cf. Jos. 24, 26b). Genesis 35, 2b[a]+4 is a secondary stratum in the story about

125

F

Clearly, the picture presented by the Pentateuch of the entire law being given to the Israelites in the desert passes neither the test of reality nor that of literature: critical examination of the various law codes in the Pentateuch testifies that they are not homogeneous and were not written in a single period. To assume that there was but one author seems implausible when we consider the three laws concerning Hebrew slaves (Ex. 21, 2-11; Lev. 25, 39-46; Dt. 15, 12-18) or the three laws about the Sabbatical year (Ex. 23, 10-11; Lev. 25, 2-7; Dt. 15, 1-11), among others. The different laws are sometimes contradictory, at other times complementary, reflecting different socio-economic situations and variegated interests in the circles of Israelite society living in the land of Israel.[32]

The law codes are not complete. In many biblical books, which are not legal in character, we find allusions to laws not mentioned in the law codes: rules of guarantee are reflected in Proverbs 6, 1ff; 20, 16, etc.; no mention of the annual sacrifice (1 Sam. 1, 21; 20, 6) is made in the Pentateuch; modes of transferring property are learned only from Jeremiah 32 and Ruth 4. Even the Pentateuch itself assumes the reader knows of other laws. Deuteronomy 24, 1-4 deals with a very exceptional

Jacob's pilgrimage to Bethel, the intent of which is to present Schechem as a site of idolatry defiled forever. Not only is the law not present under the terebinth (אלה, so we read in the Septuagint to Joshua 24, 26 and not "curse" [אָלָה] a tendentious change of the Masorites), but idols are buried there and defile the site. It is not by chance that the Septuagint adds to verse 4 the words "until this day"; see also Jubilees 31, 2. On the relationship between Joshua 24 and Genesis 35, see Y. Zakovitch, "The Tendency of the Story about the Burial of the Alien Gods in Schechem," *Beth-Mikra* (1980), pp. 30-37 (Hebrew).

32 This is one of the fundamental concepts on which biblical criticism is based. See, for instance, A. Rofé, "Ancient Israelite Law in the Light of Biblical Criticism," *Mishpatim* 13 (1984), pp. 477-482 (Hebrew).

expression of divorce law and makes clear that the general and simple law of divorce is obvious and common knowledge, making written record of it unnecessary. In the law of the maidservant we read: "And if he designated her for his son, he shall deal with her as is the practice (מִשְׁפָּט) with free maidens" (Ex. 21, 9), words which assume this practice to be common custom. Indeed, the primary meaning of the word מִשְׁפָּט is "custom." This is clear in Judges 13, 12; 2 Kings 1, 7; and especially 1 Samuel 2, 12-14: "Now Eli's sons were scoundrels; they did not know the Lord. This was the priests' practice (מִשְׁפַּט הכהנים) with the people. When anyone brought a sacrifice, the priests' boy would come along with a three-pronged fork while the meat was boiling, and he would thrust it into the cauldron, or the kettle, or the great pot or the small cooking-pot; and whatever the fork brought up, the priest would take away on it . . . " It is interesting that the word מִשְׁפָּט in this verse was later understood to mean "law," leading some Hebrew manuscripts, as well as the Greek, Syriac and Aramaic versions, to read: "Now Eli's sons . . . did not know the Lord and the due of the priests from the people" (ומשפט הכהנים מאת העם)—a different division of the two verses and a dittography of the letter מ. This reading follows Deuteronomy 18, 3: "This, then, shall be the due of the priests from the people (וזה יהיה משפט הכהנים מאת העם). Everyone who offers a sacrifice, whether an ox or a sheep, must give the shoulder, the cheeks, and the stomach to the priest . . . " The reversed text of Samuel understands the crime of Eli's sons as breaking the law which defines the priests' rights in the book of Deuteronomy.

It is highly improbable that all the laws of the Pentateuch—or even a part of them—are of the mosaic period. Numerous biblical stories demonstrate ignorance of the pentateuchal laws, such as the story of Amnon and Tamar, which supposes that marriage of a brother to his half-sister is legal (2 Sam. 13, 12-13), in disaccord with the law of Leviticus 18, 9, 11.

127

Furthermore, the many parallels between the biblical law and law codes of the ancient Near East make untenable the claim that the Israelite law was a product of a cultural vacuum.[33] While the ancient Israelites had no direct knowledge of these codes, they shared the legal heritage of the region with its neighbors (possible intermediate links between Mesopotamian law and Hebrew law have not yet been discovered). As a result, laws concerning a goring ox are recorded not only in Exodus 21, 28-32, 35-36, but also in the laws of Eshnunna (ca. 1900 B.C.E.; §53-55), and in the Laws of Hammurabi §250-252 (ca. 1750 B.C.E.), creating the unavoidable impression that this case (and not that of a kicking horse, for instance) was debated in every respectable ancient Near-Eastern law school.

The close relationship between the cultures of Israel and its neighbors is not limited to the realm of law: the Hebrew language is none other than the "language of Canaan" (Isa. 19, 18)[34] and numbers among the linguistic family of Canaanite languages along with the ancient Canaanite, Phoenician, Punic, Moabite and Amonite languages. Moreover, ancient Hebrew script was no different from Canaanite script; the script of the Gezer calendar, for example, is identical with the Phoenician script of the tenth century B.C.E.,[35] and the Moabite script in inscriptions of the eighth century reveals a considerable number of features which later, in the eighth century, became consolidated in Hebrew script.[36]

As for the literary form of Canaanite literature (the literature of the city-kingdom Ugarit), elements such as word pairs, conventional narrative formulae and patterns of the various

33   See R. Yaron (n. 16), pp. 81-84.
34   A name perhaps given to a literary language common to Israel and the other inhabitants of the land, see: M. Goshen-Gottstein, *Hebrew and Semitic Languages, An Outline Introduction*, Tel-Aviv 1965, p. 10 (Hebrew).
35   J. Naveh, *Early History of the Alphabet*, Jerusalem 1982, p. 65.
36   Ibid.

forms of parallelism, all find expression in biblical literature,[37] which developed and raised them to a higher artistic
level. This resemblance is not limited to form: many parallels
exist between Ugaritic and Mesopotamian epics and biblical
verses, parallels which help us to assemble the Israelite
"answer" to the epics of the ancient Near East.[38] The fact that
prophets, poets and sages made sophisticated use of epic
motifs and expressions, and that their figurative language is
replete with allusions to epic plots and characters, teaches us
that this type of literature was far from alien to their
audience. Biblical literature clearly struggles to purify plots
and motifs familiar to us from the region's literature, and
echoes of mythic worlds still reverberate in the Bible as well.
Thus, for example, the tradition about Enoch's miraculous disappearance (Gen. 5, 22-24) and the narrative about the sons of
God and the daughters of men (6, 1-4) find their parallels in
the literature of the cultures surrounding Israel.[39]

It is not an easy task even to delineate the border separating
the religion of Israel from the religion of Canaan.

---

37 See U. Cassuto, "Biblical and Canaanite Literature," *Biblical
and Oriental Studies*, vol. 2, Jerusalem 1975, pp. 16-59; S. E.
Loewenstamm, "Notes on the Origin of some Biblical Figures of
Speech," *M. Z. Segal Volume*, Jerusalem 1965, pp. 180-187
(Hebrew); idem, "The Seven Day Unit in Ugaritic Epic
Literature," *IEJ* 15 (1965), pp. 121-133; idem, "Remarks on
Stylistic Patterns in Biblical and Ugaritic Literatures,"
Leshonenu 32 (1968), pp. 25-36 (Hebrew); Y. Avishur, *Stylistic
Studies of Word-Pairs in Biblical and Ancient Semitic
Literatures* (AOAT 210), Neukirchen-Vluyn 1984; idem, "The
Forms of Repetition of Numbers Indicating Wholeness (3, 7, 10) in
the Bible and Ancient Semitic Literature," *Beer-Sheva* 1 (1973),
pp. 1-55 (Hebrew).
38 U. Cassuto, see above, n. 3, p. 73.
39 U. Cassuto, *Commentary on Genesis*, trans. I. Abrahams,
Jerusalem 1961, vol. 1, pp. 281-286; idem, "The Episode of the
Sons of God and the Daughters of Men (Gen. 6, 1-4)," *Biblical
and Oriental Studies* (see n. 3), pp. 17-28.

Polytheism—or something like it—was no stranger to biblical Israel. Extra-biblical sources and findings point undeniably to the active participation of the Israelites in worship of the Canaanite gods. Inscriptions painted on pottery vessels from the ninth century B.C.E. uncovered at Kuntillet 'Ajrud, for example, give the God of Israel a mate: "May you be blessed by God, who guards us and his Ashera" and "Amaryahu said to my lord . . . may you be blessed by God and by his Ashera . . . "[40]

Letters from the Jewish colony of Elephantine testify that as late as the fifth century B.C.E. the local Jews did not worship God alone: in the lists of those who served in the Temple of Yahu are theophoric names containing the appellations of pagan gods: Eshem-bethel, Anath-bethel.[41] In another document,[42] a certain Menahem bar Shalom takes an oath "by the name of [the Go]d Ya[hu] in his sanctuary and by Anathyahu."

The lack of distinction between idolatry and the worship of the God of Israel in ways not according to pentateuchal norms is discernable in the book of Deuteronomy, a book unparalleled in its sharp emphasis on the division between Israel and Canaan. In one breath, the book of Deuteronomy demands the eradication of idolatry and prescribes the proper way to worship the God of Israel: "You must destroy all the sites at which the nations you are to dispossess worshipped their gods . . . Tear down their altars, smash their pillars, put their sacred posts to the fire, and cut down the images of their gods . . . Do not worship the Lord your God in like manner, but look only to the site that the Lord your God will choose amidst all your tribes . . . There you are to go, and there you are to bring your burnt offerings and other sacrifices . . . " (12,

---

40 Z. Meshel, *Kuntillet 'Ajrud, A Religious Centre from the Time of the Judean Monarchy on the Border of Sinai*, Jerusalem 1978.
41 A. E. Cowley, *Aramaic Papyri of the Fifth Century B.C.*, Oxford 1923, nos. 21, 40.
42 Ibid., no. 44.

2-6). King Josiah's fulfillment of this demand also combines the negation of idolatry with the purification of Yahweh-worship and the centralization of the cult in Jerusalem (2 Ki. 23, 4-8).

The prohibition of idolatry appears even in the Ten Commandments (Ex. 20, 2-3), along with the ban on making images to the Lord—an illegitimate form of Yahweh worship (vss. 4-5). The different traditional divisions of the Decalogue testify to the overlapping of the two spheres and the embarrassment it engendered. The Masoretic division of the commandments separates "I the Lord am your God . . ." from the commandment: "You shall have no other gods besides Me," which itself includes "You shall not make for yourself a sculptured image, or any likeness of what is in the heavens above, or on the earth below, or in the waters under the earth." According to the Masoretic formulation, the sculptured image is a form of idolatry. Philo Alexandrinus and some of the church fathers, on the other hand, preserve a division which combines "I the Lord am your God . . . " and "You shall have no other gods besides me"—that is, the prohibition of idolatry—and places "You shall not make for yourself any sculptured image . . . " by itself, as dealing with the improper worship of Yahweh.

Even Baal worship, considered by the prophets as blatant idolatry, might possibly be a displaced expression of worship of the God of Israel. The prophet Hosea himself, for example, says: "And in that day, declares the Lord—you will call [Me] Ishi (i.e., my husband, lit. 'my man') and no more will you call me Baali (i.e., my Baal [master])" (Ho. 2, 18). Consider, as well, the free variation of the names Baal and Yah(weh) in the etiological explanation of the place name of David's victory, "Baal-perazim": "For Yahweh has broken through my enemies before me as waters break through" (2 Sam. 5, 20). The appearance of different theophoric names containing the element 'Baal'—Jerubaal (Jud. 6, 32), Ishbaal (1 Chr. 8, 33), Meribaal (1 Chr. 8, 34)—seems to testify that the name 'Baal' was a name of the God of Israel which, at a certain time and in

131

certain circles, was unobjectionable. Moreover, the temple, which in Judges 9, 4 is called "the temple of Baal-berith," is, later on in the same chapter, referred to as "the temple of El-berith" (vs. 46).

These examples make manifestly clear that Israel is a legitimate child of the Canaanite culture. In order to differentiate between the Israelite monotheistic element and the idolatrous Canaanite environment, the Bible frequently resorts to expressing an utter rejection of Canaan. An example of this is the curse of Canaan in Genesis 9, 25: "Cursed be Canaan; the lowest of slaves shall he be to his brothers."

The literature of the Former Prophets provides two accounts of the conquest and settlement of the land by the Israelites. One of these, in the book of Joshua, presents the victory almost as a campaign of exhilarating military blitzes, with divine assistance delivering the nations and their kings into the hands of the Israelites. According to this tradition, contacts between the Israelites and the Canaanites who escaped annihilation were fleeting and sporadic, occurring as a result of the Israelites' disobedient failure to avoid any traffic with the local population (see for instance Dt. 7, 1-6). The second account of the conquest, found in the first chapter of the book of Judges, paints a less rosy picture. It recounts failure after failure of the conquest: the Israelites had more non-conquests than conquests and as a result were forced to dwell among the not dispossessed Canaanite population. For example: "Manasseh did not dispossess [the inhabitants of] Beth-shean and its dependencies, or [of] Taanach and its dependencies, or the inhabitants of Dor and its dependencies, or the inhabitants of Ibleam and its dependencies, or the inhabitants of Megiddo and its dependencies. The Canaanites persisted in dwelling in this region. And when Israel gained the upper hand, they subjected the Canaanites to forced labor, but they did not dispossess them. Nor did Ephraim dispossess the Canaanites who inhabited Gezer; so the Canaanites dwelt in their midst at Gezer" (vss. 27-29). Even though the first chapter of Judges is clearly biased in its account of the conquest (it seeks to enhance the image of the tribe of Judah who did its proper duty, in contrast to the remaining tribes who failed in their mission), it is nonetheless a more realistic portrayal than its counterpart in the book of Joshua. According to Judges 1, Israel dwells among the Canaanite population. While the picture portrayed in Judges is more realistic than that in Joshua, it remains incomplete. We would go one step further: the people of Israel are comprised primarily of the indigenous inhabitants of the land: Canaanites themselves.

G

The intimate relationship between the children of Israel and the Canaanites necessitated the reinforcement and intensification of the Exodus myth, the belief that the people of Israel were created in Egypt and received their law and culture in the wilderness. The development and acceptance of the monotheistic faith was undoubtedly slow and painful, but the Bible presents this faith as second nature to Israel. Monotheism accompanies the people of Israel from the moment God said to Abraham: "Go forth from your native land and from your father's house . . . " (Gen. 12, 1) and from the day the Law was given to Israel, and the whole people heard the words: "I the Lord am your God who brought you out of the land of Egypt, the house of bondage" (Ex. 20, 2). The myth of the Exodus was created in order to encourage the Israelites to accept the revolution of monotheism and to believe that they make up an exceptional creation completely different from the nations surrounding them: "There is a people that dwells apart, not reckoned among the nations" (Nu. 23, 9).

Index of Biblical References

135